Copyright and Disclosure Notice

Disclosure Statement

"Now That Makes Me Mad^{sm}...About Politics" by Dr. Keith A. Robinson, published by *Spines Publishing*, is a work of political satire. The book utilizes fictional characters, fictional stories, and photographs of public personalities and politicians. The opinions and assertions expressed within are satirical and opinion in nature and solely those of the author.

The intent of this book is to entertain the public and to motivate readers and listeners to participate in the legal casting of votes reflective of their chosen political affiliation. The content is not intended to defame, malign, or libel any individual, race, group, or entity.

With the exception of the author and book dedication recipients, all characters and events depicted in this book are fictitious. Any resemblance to actual persons, living or dead, or actual events is purely coincidental. The use of names and photographs of public personalities and politicians is for illustrative, entertainment, and satirical purposes only.

ISBN: 979-8-89383-965-4

Contents

Chapter One

Book Dedication

During the writing of this book, four people constantly whispered thoughts, ideas, and stories into my head. Their whispers erupted as words and stories in this book. These four giants in my life must be remembered, for they changed my life into my current form and personality. To these four, I dedicate this book.

Mary Lou Robinson (Alley) 1923-2014 'My Sweet Mama'

Bennie J. Robinson
1923-2002 "My Daddy"

I have been blessed beyond measure by a wonderful mother and father chosen for just me by Almighty God. They touched my life from the beginning with love, guidance, and creativity. I am so thankful that, even as a writer, words can't express my love and respect for their parenting.

Lorn H. Robinson 1921-2010
"My Papa Lorn"

Papa Lorn was my second dad. He taught me about "snakes" (both on the ground and walking upright). Snakes need to be kept at a distance or put in a box so they won't hurt anyone. To my Papa Lorn, thanks for the love and wisdom for life. This book reveals so much about our lives and your wisdom.

Dr. Thomas White, Ph.D
. (Quantum Physicist) Navy
SEAL (Ret) 1948-present

"Brother from a different mother"

Brother Tom has known me longer than anyone other than God or my parents. Years after leaving Midwest City, Oklahoma, I found my buddy Tommy (actually, he found me.) Moving to Texas and the Vietnam War has a way of separating buddies who grew up together and were invisibly joined at the heart. This is a man of wisdom, a man who was ready to give his life for others. I can't say enough about Tom's sacrifices for America and Americans. Because of his lifelong friendship, wisdom, and strength of character, I am compelled to dedicate this book to his life of service and our never-ending friendship.

Chapter Two

Foreword

Foreword

"Why me? Why not me?" Like many, I find myself increasingly disillusioned and, quite frankly, "raging mad" at the condition of our world today.

I am Dr. Thomas White, Ph.D., Quantum Physicist. My work involves understanding the universe's behavior at the smallest scale—atoms, electrons, and photons. It's our job to test the rules of this quantum world and push their boundaries. However, I never expected to encounter smaller particles in our societal fabric until I started listening to certain political leaders currently running our country. I've found that their ideas often seem to represent the tiniest particles of rational thought. This realization makes me "raging mad." No one stretches the boundaries of reason more than the current political regime.

Dr. Keith Robinson and I have been friends for over 65 years. I consider him a brother, chaplain, advisor, and one of the kindest men

I know. We grew up in church together, blessed with the best parents who taught us enduring life lessons. Back then, we weren't mad.

Coming from a military background in Special Forces, I served for 14 years before being medically retired. I've seen the best and worst of men and have been a patriot all my life. My family has served this country since the 18th century. There was a saying from my time: "My Country, right or wrong." We stood strong and dedicated, not only to our country but to anyone in need of our support.

Today, that sentiment seems lost in the current political landscape, and that makes me "raging mad."

During my time as a SEAL, I worked in over 54 countries and lived in 18, gaining insights into diverse cultures and governance. Now, we find ourselves under a form of governance unlike anything we've seen in our country. So, I do have an attitude? You can bet on it! I'm not only "mad" but "sad" as well.

Dr. Robinson's insight and passion for this country, combined with his ability to express his thoughts with humor, agitation, and anger, is refreshing and poignant. His work, "Now That Makes Me Madsm...about Politics," humorously yet directly addresses the heart and soul of the American people.

Join him on this journey and know it's alright to be mad; you are not alone. Welcome to the MAD WORLD in which we now find ourselves. Hopefully, we can cope and find our way back. Dr. Keith has shown us the path—now let's do something about it.

Dr.Thomas M. White, Ph.D

President/CEO/Founder iVest International, LLC,

CloudEvac Technologies, LLC - Link2 Life Foundation, LLC

312-339-6342 Cell

tom@ivested.net drtom@cloudevac.com

*****END*****

Chapter Three

Author Introduction:

Author Introduction

Why Do I Need Skin?

It was a typical day in the clinic. Patients were in the reception room, and after answering emails, it was time to see my first patient: an 85-year-old man with gray, thinning hair and squinting eyes. After I shook his hand, I asked, " What can I do for you, sir?"

There was a long pause in his answer. His eyes appeared to look through me rather than at mine. He struggled to find the words for his answer.

"Doctor, I think I need you to remove my skin."

With that response, I knew this would be a challenging patient to please.

"Sir, please tell me why you think you can survive without your skin. Your skin protects you from all the foreign pathogens that try to invade your body, make you sick,or, without even knowing it, you can transmit invisible diseases to your family. Let me put it this way: with the protection of your skin, you and your family have a better chance at life. Without skin and the border protection of your body, you could die. Your life has a chance at survival with the protection of your skin. That's the way God planned it."

"Death" is a Symptom of a much bigger problem.

Medically speaking, it's true: Doctors try their best to prevent death and disability. But when the human system is pushed too far; it often ends in death or preventable disability. When death or disability occurs, there is still one more question that must be asked: Why?

In this book, we will examine the symptoms of "failure" in our political system through 'satirical eyes.' We do this intending to prevent the death ordisability of the patient: America.

Three basic political attitudes of thought

When you look at populations striving to live together in quasi-peace, harmony, and productivity, there appear to be three primary groupings of thought: ***Liberalism, Conservativism***, and ***Confusion***. I realize "confusion" can creep into the other two categories, resulting in "bedlam" and "strife." We all know what "strife" is, but our old friend, the dictionary, helps us by clarifying the definition of"bedlam": 1) *a scene of uproar and confusion and 2) an institution for the care of mentally ill people.* Sounds like we're sneaking up on a better understanding of things already.

To simplify things a bit, it looks like Conservatives spend most of their lives trying to deal with the "confusion" and "hysteria" of Liberals, while Liberals do what they can get away with and call it "Liberalism" (even if what they 'can get away with' isn't working or is outright destructive and life-threatening to the patient: America).

Let's work with that definition throughout the book and see if we are totally confused at the end. The result of taking this satirical journey with me in ***Now That Makes Me Mad^{sm}...about Politics*** will result in either a heightened commitment to the logic of Conservatism or screaming bedlam of Liberal confusion, which will never change. (I realize you may have a different definition of this topic).

<u>Stated:</u> If you're a Conservative or in a state of confusion seeking a better understanding of the forces at work in our political lives, read on. But, if you are a confirmed, died-in-the-wool Liberal, give this book to someone else.

There we go, and a path has appeared. Now, let's begin the journey.

To help frame the strength of satire in persuasive communication, I will insert targeted original political cartoons created through the artistry of a talented Chicago political cartoonist named Diane Hensley. Effective satire is genuinely a team event.

The most important issue in the upcoming election for a new President/Vice President and Congress is 'The Border Integrity of the United States.'

Ever since President Joe Biden's contested election almost four years ago, the concept of Southern Border Security has been flipped on its back. The doors leading to Mexico swung open, and by 'edict' (Presidential Proclamation), all of the stability of our national borders instantly vanished as the President sprinkled bait, attracting a massive influx of illegal aliens into America from across the world.

Texas Governor Abbott has been at the forefront of protecting the US/Mexico border. Although he is wheelchair-bound, he has represented Texas and the US intelligently, honorably, and aggressively in ways that our current President and Secretary of Homeland Security have long abandoned.

The Southern Border states began to choke at the constant stream of foreign aliens who raced across the border and disappeared into the inner sanctum of America. Trained by cartels and anxious to expand their trafficking of men, women, and children into a new form of slavery, billions of dollars began flooding into the pockets of those who controlled the borders of The United States. There was an almost symbiotic relationship formed where cartels for a massive price would deliver the new slaves to the border, where Border Patrol had has been transformed into human registration "Welcome Personnel."

Between 10 million and 13 million aliens plus "gotaways" entered America illegally...but with the Presidential Proclamation in place, they became "quasi-legal." Everyone had learned the proper verbiage to regurgitate to Border Patrol Agents, bend the rules, and become seekers of "asylum."

Still with the memory of the horrors of 9/11 fresh in the minds of lawful citizens, the masses of illegals, now on the interior of America with an asylum court date 5-8 years into the future, many of the aliens began to amass in large numbers on the streets and sidewalks of border states leaving a trail of garbage and destruction to the properties they crossed as they infiltrated America. The property was destroyed. Livestock was killed and eaten. Murders and rapes were commonplace. And then, the cry rang out from this invasion of masses, "Death to America." Illegal aliens may have believed they were escaping to freedom. but in truth, they were escaping into a new form of slavery.

In Washington DC, politicians looked on, and some even provided legal cover in hopes that thedemographic change would shift the balance of power into a landslide win forDemocrats who continued throwing money at the invasion, and the illegal alienskept coming. With costs now breaking the banks of even those enablingthe illegal influx, the President, Vice President, and democratically ledSenate quietly kept printing money that would never be paid back. And the illegal aliens kept coming from across the globe. Even our enemies sent hordes of their worstcitizens and freshly released convicts...to occupy America. What magic number would shift the balance ofpower permanently into the hands of Democrats?

Even sanctuary cities could no longer afford the perks of illegal alien status. Yet, amidst the backdrop of an upcoming election, massive inflation, and low polling numbers, Democrats continued baiting the trap for an even more significant mass migration of illegals.

How do we awaken a nation being victimized by our politicians?

It's a pretty bleak picture, but not without hope. The real question is: What is the best way to awaken the Republican conservative populace and empower them to prepare for the battle at the ballot box that is just over the horizon?

Let me be perfectly open about the intention behind this book. First, in your hands is a new information tool that might make a difference and shift the tide away from Democrats/Liberals and those sitting on the political fence. Second, this book has been designed to take you on a transformational journey, an awakening of your commitment to America.

The secret tool you hold is called political satire. This tool sometimes allows us to laugh at our opponents and the stupid things they often do that hurt our country. There is a whole lot of healing needed in our country, but the first thing we must do is get the low-down, dirty pig-stealers out of the office where they can't destroy what's left of our country. And, if possible, have a little fun along the way.

So, please refrain from forming a pre-judgment about how we unfold the topics, the stories, the passion, and the reality of what we must do to save our country for our children and us. Come along for the rideand listen to how your heart resonates with the message.

Dr. Ulyses Stuckum and I will be your guides as together as we wade through the gator-infested waters filled with Democrats/liberals feeding on what's left of America. Don't worry; there's enough left to bring America back to greatness. We can do this together but don't tell the Democrats, or they may try to mess it up. Yet, never underestimate the lengths to which Democrats will go to have their way with what's left of America.

They're supposed to be our "American brothers and sisters." Well, they can be that, but first, their power must be neutralized so they can't hurt Americans who can save this patient who might be terminally ill. So, let's get after this. It's not going to be easy, so get your boots on and get ready to take on the Democrat who talks out of all three sides of their mouths.

Biases

To tackle this book's subject matter,we need to provide some basic information about the authors and their human biases because you will see our biases throughout these upcoming pages. Dr. Ulyses Stuckum can speak for himself or not.

Biases are not inherently good or bad, but they are very real. It's safe to say that there is not one person on this earth without *biases*, and we accumulate them throughout life. They are like colored plastic gels that are invisible. They're in front of our eyes, and they filter the data input coming into our brains. Biases create our protection mechanisms. We need them to emotionally survive the journey of being human and dealing with the ups and downs of life. Our *biases* translate into our *actions*.

In the knock-down, drag-out, often unpredictable 'blood sport' known as "politics," our minds and responses must be fine-tuned for minute-by-minute changes involving attack, defense, research, and preparation for a political opponent's unknown moves ...or *lies*.

Bias Series #1

First, I am a Christian, Texan, and conservative through and through. I am a retired doctor who trained at the ***VA*** Medical Center in Los Angeles and then completed an American Cancer Society Fellowship at the University of Texas MD Anderson Cancer Hospital .My official specialty was as a Maxillofacial Prosthodontist, sculpting facial prostheses for people who had cancer or trauma involving the head and neck structures.

Bias Series #2

I am an ordained Certified Crisis Chaplain and a Diplomate in the *American Academy of Experts in Traumatic Stress*. I have also been a police chaplain and a former Chaplain with the ***Billy Graham Rapid Response Team/Samaritan's Purse*** organization.

Bias Series #3

One of my greatest joys involves the creation of stories as a screenwriter that come alive on television and in movies. My sweet wife, Brenda, and I team-write together, specializing in Christmas Dramas, Thrillers, and dramatic stories that awaken the soul and tingle the emotions. In the past, I was the screenwriter and Co-Producer of a multiple *Emmy Award-winning TV series* titled ***The Brutal Truth: A Violence Documentary and The Brutal Truth: Protecting the Family from Violence***, which aired on CBS. As a lyric tenor, I spent some wonderfully creative time performing with my singing partner onstage in the halls of Congress on *National Organ Donor Awareness Day*. Also, we recorded a musical album about the ups and downs of relationships titled ***The Stages of Our Love.***

On the cover, we see a "Proud Liberal Democrat" underwater and extremely confused. That's pretty much where we are today in the current political fight. While some segments of the book use humor, rest assured we are going to stretch the boundaries using satire. I hope that the satirical communication style in this book will get down to your heart and communicate your inner feelings about the dangers in our country and our choices for leadership.

Bias Series #4

My good friend (Carrie Woliver) and I created and performed a nationally syndicated health radio talk show and hosted over 150 episodes. Humor began finding its way into my radio performances and lectures/presentations I made before audiences. And then, I wrote a book titled ***Growing Older with Your Teeth...or Something Like Them***. It was claimed to be the first time that humor was used to carry the often-boring job of communicating health information and having people remember the subject matter. People loved the humor, and I was asked to be a national spokesperson for

Proctor & Gamble, traveling the US and performing television and radio interviews about my book...because of humor.

I've learned that humor helps sweep away many negative emotions associated with studying emotionally charged subjects that often impact our lives deeply, such as politics.

So, what do we do with President Biden?

Currently, America (Democrats, Republicans, and people unsure of their political preferences) is in the throes of electing a new president and deciding how America should be positioned in the world. After the election is over, it won't be over. The lawsuits will start, and the country will struggle with the election outcome. So, what's in this book will live on far past this election. For now, both (or possibly multiple) parties draw informational plans to show how their chosen candidate is the best for the job and why the other person in the race is a *low-down, ornery, lying, cheating pig-stealer.* (Earlier, I mentioned that I am from Texas.) There is an old story that might help right now.

Pitching Poop

As the story goes, when kids grew up on the farm or ranch, they had to be pretty creative about the games they could play and not get hurt too badly. Those early games became the basis for the sport of Rodeo, but they can be somewhat dangerous.

Because of all the livestock that they had, many piles of poop littered the ground. And, needing some way to pass the time (and have a little fun) found out that if you picked the right pile of poop at the right time, you could pick it up and throw it great distances. There was a steep learning curve on the art of *poop throwing.* The poop had to be really dry, or you were left with a stinky mess on your hands...and the poop wouldn't go very far.

Politics involves *Poop-throwing*

I believe that much of the *poop-throwing* you see during today's political elections had its earliest start from those days of throwing poop on the farm or ranch. I must say, today's politicians (both Republicans and Democrats often termed "Republicrats") are superb at the art of "poop throwing." (We don't tell Democrats about the need for the poop to be very dry. Many Democrats haven't figured out the secret yet.)

News organizations and misguided, biased, hate-driven news hosts on TV are masterful *poop throwers,* but they haven't spent much time on the farm/ranch, and they keep trying to throw *fresh poop,* thinking it will help the candidate that they want to win. They have entire teams of *'stinky poop specialists'* out in public, turning over rocks, going into family backgrounds, and looking for pictures of the opposing candidate with poop on their hands to sling in all directions on their quasi-news shows. They revel at finding a new pile of poop. Quite possibly, the enemy candidate was seen boarding the plane of a deceased pedophile for a trip to a hidden island. Fresh poop.

In so many ways, the media and their pundits have damaged the mental DNA of our people because of confusion about their jobs of reporting on the news. Rather than presenting the facts about a political story, they become a part of the story by picking a side and only showing a hidden bias they will never admit. These mutated news "professionals" think the viewing public is stupid and take advantage of that perceived stupidity through the power of the media. Listen up news media: ***America doesn't need you to pre-digest life for us.*** Give us the facts and let the public make their own decisions. At least in this book, I give you the biases up front.

Some candidates secretly try to get the poop before large audiences, and it ends up on "The View." These folks really know *poop* but are ashamed about what to do with it. The hosts and producers on "The

View" have mastered ***poopology*** and may have advanced degrees in this specialty, but missed all the classes on "ethics in the media." And, yep, they wear it home every day after trying to spread the poop to audiences who believe their opinions about *poop*. Quite often, as they are slinging fresh *poop*, they realize that it's their own *poop*. Americans don't need media poop, and there's enough *poop* in the real world in which we live.

Ok, let's take a peek at what just happened.

Using humor, we created a means by which we can have fun with stinky subjects and yet communicate a message about politics and the battle style therein. And, after spending a little time with the poop-throwing story, you will probably never be able to watch "The View" without thinking about the *poop* they are trying to throw on the public and how it is landing on them.

So, the next time you catch a politician pitching *poop*, you may need to help them realize what they are doing. Call it like it is and say one word nice and loud, "Poop." (Oh, by the way, as you do this, you may not want to stand behind people. They may think you're yelling a "command" rather than stating your opinion.)

Chapter Four

Author Introduction: (SPLIT)

The Presumption of Truth: The demand for those in public office

Americans want to believe and expect their elected officials to tell them the truth. Even though history has shown that this doesn't always happen, Americans really shouldn't need to slap down a Bible and have an elected official keep his/her hand on it as they speak. If they speak, it should be the truth.

But, just like my young awakening when I discovered that *Mickey Mouse*® was a fictional character and *Popeye*® didn't really eat mountains of spinach, little minds like to believe the truth happens spontaneously. At some point, people begin thinking it's ok to bend the truth without letting the audience know. As a fiction writer, I always bend the truth to make the story work. Yes, in this book, I've created some twists and turns to make the story serve its purpose. You will figure them out probably by the end of the book.

I was preparing to receive my doctorate diploma at the graduation ceremony. Before we left for the stadium, where 150 of us were to receive our training certification and become *doctors*, I briefly talked with my mom, a relatively unpredictable sweetheart whose heart was very proud of her baby.

"Mom, you're not going to do anything out of the ordinary, are you? With a look of total innocence, she assured me, "No." With her assurance, we headed to the massive stadium, where the provost delivered his final words of wisdom for this batch of new doctors about to be released to the public.

"Learn something new every day. You are going into "Practice" to help your fellow man and woman. If you do this, you will have given twenty to thirty years of your life to helping folks when you retire. That's good. If you don't do this, you will only have one year of practice that you have repeated twenty to thirty times. If you do the latter, you should have never been conferred the degree of *doctor*."

Since "Robinson" was in the back half of the alphabetized mass when I walked across that stage to pick up my diploma, I still recall how my mom stood up in the audience with her plastic camera and yelled, "Turn this way, baby."

The provost put his arm around my shoulder and whispered, "Son, this is not the first time this has happened. She is proud of you. This is her moment, too." We smiled together, and she snapped the picture. Somewhat red-faced, I walked off the stage. Many years after retirement from practice, I knew Mom and Dad were always proud of their only baby boy doctor. She had told me a fib, and in my heart, I knew something was coming that day.

Everything changes once someone is elected to office.

When elected to a distinguished public office, whether the President of the United States or the Fixer of Potholes in a small town, the day you start your service as an elected official, **you should commit yourself to telling the truth to the people who elected you.** You work for "them/us," not the other way around.

One day, I was interviewing Texas Lt. Governor Dan Patrick after being elected.

My question to the new Texas Lt.Governor of Texas was this: "Many starry-eyed intelligent people get themselves elected and head off to lead the people. Then something happens - they forget the promises they made to get there. How will you keep your promises as our new Lt. Governor of Texas?"

Dan smiled and said, "Dr. Robinson, you raise an important question. Here's how you will help me remember my promises. If I break a promise or get off track for being a good leader, you can call me during my weekly radio talk show and remind me...on the air. Will you do that for me? My response was: "Yes, sir, I will." I have never had to make that call.

Lt Governor Dan Patrick has kept his promises to me and Texas. He and Governor Greg Abbott know their jobs and are dedicated to their jobs in Texas. One day, we will see their names in higher positions in our federal government. But for now, Texas is honored to have them in their jobs as Governor and Lt. Governor of our state. These two Texas leaders tell the truth and are dedicated to keeping Texans safe during this open border fiasco created by the Biden/Harris fiasco administration. Happily, the political cartoon shown above paints a picture of our border. Governor Abbott, in his wheelchair symbolically, had confronted President Biden over the border. Even though a falling tree took away the Governor's ability to walk, Abbott wins and is gone in a flash.

Sadly, not all elected officials do what is "right" and make some really bad choices.

I'm not sure our elected officials know this tiny, but very important commitment to 'doing what is right.' Yet, almost every day, we find another misguided elected official going down in flames for lying and doing really stupid things. What mother and father want to say to the news camera, "Our son/daughter was the best "liar" ever elected to public office...he/she was just caught at it."

Some of our elected officials could have starred in the live re-enactment of the iconic show "Liar, Liar." Jim Carey was brilliant in playing an attorney whose young son saw through his lies and asked for a miracle. For 24 hours, his dad could not tell a lie—not one. The audience saw the tragedy when a man who lied at the drop of a hat without shame became bound by the miracle that he had to tell the truth.

Every elected official should be required to watch the show "Liar, Liar" before taking office—any office.

What motivates people to do anything?

Only two motivations cause humans to change: 1) humans move toward events that bring them *pleasure*, and 2) humans move away from events that bring them *pain*.

After *Pomp and Circumstance* music ended and reality began in an elected position, one would think that the elected person would gravitate naturally to make the public who elected them *proud*. For many elected people, that is exactly what they do. For others, a bucket of stinky slime begins to filter into the evacuated space that used to hold their brains, and they begin believing they are above the people who elected them. They are more intelligent than the people who elected them. Those 'little people' who elected them are no longer their employers; they are now just "subjects to be used, abused, and taxed into oblivion." They believe that the only purpose of being elected ...is to be re-elected. And the only way to perpetuate the limelight position of power they now hold...is to lie, hide, and cheat.

The real sign that they are headed for an embarrassing awakening by those stupid people who voted for them is that...they begin to believe the verbal *poop* coming out of their mouths and think that the public can't see it.

The Mayorkian Red Hand Award

This entire book is about "opinions" based on "perceptions" of people's <u>actions</u>. While it is still legal, we're talking about **opinions.** But now it's time for a change...big change. I propose that elected officials who *lie* and are discovered as *committed liars* are forced to undergo what I term the ***Mayorkian Red Hand Award***. (It sounds like something from a Star Trek movie...but it isn't. Let me explain this proposed "Award.")

The term ***caught red-handed*** referred to *the blood on the hands of a villain*. But ***red-handed*** also should be awarded for much more than just being caught with your hands in the proverbial *cookie jar*. Lying while in public office must be raised to its rightful position of *public disgrace* with more than just words of shame and disgust. Many politicians have developed a very thick skin, capable of widespread public disgrace because of repeated lying, which doesn't seem to bother them.

The public needs to be able to spot who has a repeated history of lying to America and Americans. For those public liars, the right hand that they raise to swear their *Oath of Office* and that they raise swearing to *tell the truth, the whole truth,* and *nothing but the truth* is where the coveted **Mayorkian Red Hand** award is placed.

America has creative inventors who can formulate a wonderfully flexible, candy apple red epoxy that sticks to the skin and will not come off for at least four years. This Mayorkian red epoxy would be painted onto the palm and fingers of just one side of the right hand of a known elected or appointed *public liar*.

Words disappear into the air, leaving only their negative effect on the public and the country's people. The **Mayorkian Red Handed Award** lasts so that *liars* can be given the appropriate honor they so richly have earned and be spotted at a safe distance. In that way, you can know if their lips are moving...they're probably lying.

The World's Biggest LiarContest

If you go to Wikipedia free encyclopedia and look up "World's Biggest Liar" this is what you will find. (https://en.wikipedia.org/wiki/Worl d%27s_Biggest_Liar)

"World's BiggestLiar is an annual competition for telling lies, held in Cumbria, England.Competitors from around the world have five minutes to tell the biggest and most convincing lie they can.[1] Competition rules bar the use of props or scripts. Politicians and lawyers are not allowed to enter the competition, because "they are judged to be too skilled at telling porkies".[2]

History

TheWorld's Biggest Liar competition is held every November at the Bridge Inn, SantonBridge,in memory of Will Ritson (1808–1890), a pub landlord[3]from Wasdale, who was well known forhis "tall-tales".[4] One of Ritson'smost famous fibs was that turnips grew so large inthe LakeDistrict thatpeople carved them out to make cow s heds.[4]

Recent competitions

In 2003, Abrie Krueger of South Africa was named the world's biggest liar after telling a story about how he was crowned King of the Wasdale Valley. This marked the first time that a foreigner had won the competition, which was marked with allegations of Krueger having cheated.[5] A Bishop of Carlisle[6] was supposed to have once won the competition with the shortest-ever speech; he simply said, "I have never told a lie in my life."[7]

Comedian Sue Perkins won the competition in 2006, marking the first time in the event's history that a woman won the competition.[1] Her winning tall tale was about how the ozone layer became damaged, icecaps melted and people had to be taken to work on cam els.[1]

In 2008, John "Johnny Liar" Graham won the competition for the seventh time after telling the judges a story of a magical ride to Scotland in a wheelie bin that went under the sea.[4] The previous year Graham's winning lie was that a World War II German submarine had invaded Britain to capture digitaltelevision decoders.[2]

PaulBurrows from Essex won the competition in 2010. He told a story of how the lakes and mountains of the Cumbrian countryside had been stolen from the county of Essex, leaving it as flat as it is today.[8]

The 2011 winner was Glen Boylan. His story involved betting on a snail race with Prince Charles (who advised him to remove the shell to make it more aerodynamic) and losing because his opponents cheated with battery-operated snails.[9][10]

2013 saw Mike Naylor win for the third time of his Lying career. Naylor, a 57-year-old man from Wasdale, told a story about Wassie, the monster that lives in Wastwater, the local lake.[11] He is the nephew of JossNaylor, better known as a fell runner, but himself also a former winner of the competition.[12]

In 2019, Phillip Gate from Workington won with a story about how Cumbria is rich not only in coal deposits but also sugar, which is the reason for the county large jam production.[13]

References

1.   *"Comedienne crownedbiggest liar". BBC. 16 November 2006. Retrieved 22November 2008.*

2.   *"No, honestly,'world's biggest liar' crowned". China Daily. 17 November 2007.Retrieved 22 November 2008.*

3.   *"Santon Bridge Inn". Santonbridgeinn.com.Retrieved 24 October 2021.*

4.   *"King Liar holds onto his crown". BBC. 21 November 2008.Retrieved 22 November 2008.*

5.   *Ahmed, Maria (28November 2003). "World's biggestliar accused of cheating". London: Times Online. Retrieved 26November 2008.*

6.   *"Cumberland andWestmorland Herald; Letters, 19 October 2007". Retrieved 24October 2021.*

7.   *Wainwright,Martin (21 November 2007). "Who's the world'sbiggest liar?". London: Guardian.co.uk. Retrieved 24November 2008.*

8.   *Cleaver, Alan(19 November 2010). "World's BiggestLiar Crowned". London: Independent.co.uk. Archived from the original on 24 November2010. Retrieved 16 January 2011.*

9.   *AlistairMacDonald (25 November 2011). "Honestly, This Partof England Has the World's Biggest Liars". The Wall StreetJournal. Retrieved 7 December 2011.*

10.   *"I've only been inone of the creme de la creme liars since I became a supervisor at Sellafield.Now I'm having to deal with lots of expert liars all the time...'". News & Star. 21November 2011. Retrieved 7 December 2011.*

11.   *"Ballet star showsoff charity portraits". Bucks Free Press. Retrieved 24October 2021.*

12.   *Mike Amos (13April 2011). "Ad lib, adfib".The Northern Echo. Retrieved 28 June 2015.*

13.   *Pidd, Helen (22November 2019). "Festival of fibs: Workington Man is crowned world's biggest liar". The Guardian.Retrieved 26 September 2020*

(I have included the references for this Wikipedia article so you can check out the citations(and so you'll know I'm not lying about this dubious competition.)

Lying has been around for along time

Yes, lying has existed for a long time, possibly since the *Garden of Eden*. As the story goes on, Adam lies to God about how it is Eve's fault that he ate the apple. (It's always the woman's fault, right?) Remember, this is a satire/humor book.

How have humans twisted lying into something some consider *good and easy*? How can some minds believe that lies will never be discovered by the people you never want to discover them? (Intergalactic Truth: They always find it out, and then you find it out when it hits the International News circuit on TikTok, Facebook, Instagram, or Fox News.)

I believe that liars may have a genetic predisposition to twisting the truth. Suppose you look back in the liar's DNA or family. In that case, you might find that as a child growing up, the liar either watched some family member partake of the lying conundrum and said in the mind of the child, *If mom and/or dad can lie... then it must be ok for me to do that too...* or if the child tried lying and wasn't stopped when they were discovered. Without that, I suggest they received tacit approval that *lying was OK*. Instantly, that *permission to lie* was plated into the DNA where it hid, growing in strength for later fateful use in life.

So, this may be the origin of the problem. Why did the Creator of the Universe put **Thou shall not lie** in the top ten rules for life? But reality reminds us that it's a problem many, if not all, humans grapple with at some point in their lives, especially if that individual is in politics.

Does it make you wonder why, when someone is called before a congressional committee, the witness must swear to tell the truth and can go to jail if they lie, but the Congressmen and women in the same room are <u>not sworn in as well</u>? And they lie all over the place with no consequences.

Does it make you wonder how our elected officials (Congressmen, women, and Senators) can deliver a 2000-page bill/law filled with so much pork that it makes the pig ashamed...on the night before the vote...and our officially elected representative never reads one word of the bill before voting? Our representatives are the elected ones, not their staff, who are unelected.

How about this: before <u>any vote on any bill</u> in the House of Representatives or Senate, the elected official must swear that he or she has personally read every word of the bill and "under the penalty of perjury before Congress" must affirm they have done so, or their vote doesn't count? I like that one.

As you can see, we will 'slap some hornet nests' in the chapters ahead, stirring up those bad boys and girls. But look at where we are now. Sometimes, you have to slap that hornet's nest and then run like there is no tomorrow.

America can't continue on the path that knowingly leads to failure and chaos. What kind of an America will we leave to our children and grandchildren if we don't take this seriously?

(By the way, if you are a Democrat/Liberal and rereading this book, let me say this again...hand it to someone else. You have been warned!)

So, let's get at this...and have some fun along the way...if possible.

Dr. Keith A. Robinson

End...beginning

Chapter Five

"Meet Dr. Stuckum"

Chapter 1

"Meet Dr. Stuckum"

Dr. Ulyses Stuckum - West
Texas Media Personality

As a Texas doctor with a Nationally syndicated health radio talk show titled "*America Talks Health*℠ *with Dr. Keith*

Robinson," I've always been fascinated with different communication techniques.

I've pondered what creative ways can help people learn things about their bodies, which will get them to voluntarily listen and retain information about colonoscopies, toe fungus, or the ravages of gum disease. After several years of experience, I've realized there's only one thing that could willingly connect a layman with any medical jargon (or other jargon), which is humor.

Working with the famous heart surgeon Dr Michael E. DeBakey, MD, at the *Houston Methodist Hospital* gave me great opportunities to meet and interview some of the finest medical minds across the globe.

Joking with your heart surgeon

One day, as Dr. DeBakey and a herd of his young doctors were making "rounds" to see the progress or decline in their patients' medical condition or prepare them for heart surgery or transplant, I got to see the master communicator, Dr. DeBakey, interact with a patient about to receive a new heart.

The man was understandably nervous but attempted to catch Dr. DeBakey off guard with a moment of humor.

"Dr. DeBakey, is there a guarantee that comes with my new heart?"

Without missing a beat (no pun intended), Dr. DeBakey smiled at the gentleman and responded, "Yes sir, there is... it's a lifetime guarantee on this one."

At that moment, communication occurred through humor. Then Dr. DeBakey took the hand of the man and said, "I'm going to take good care of you, but you're lucky... this is not my first transplant."

Both men smiled, filled with new insight about their relationship.

Later, Dr. DeBakey honored me by writing the medical foreword to my first book, titled *"**Growing Older with Your Teeth, or something like them**."*

The point is that everyone loves humor and uses it to lighten difficult situations or simplify otherwise tricky topics. It's why you often witness so many memes about political matters all across social media.

People often use humor to vocalize their frustrations and opinions funnily. The clever ones take it one step ahead and spotlight the poop the politicians have been hurling our way for others to see beyond the windshield so caked with political poop there's no chance that they will ever see the truth.

However, out of all those Smart Alecs, no one is quite as witty and clever as good ol' Dr. Stuckum.

How I found Dr. Ulyses Stuckum

Long ago, I used to drive a lot more than I do today. I was invited to speak at a meeting in West Texas. While driving through the vast, uninhabited parts with a never-ending road only frequented by a rabbit or Texas Speed Bump (armadillo), I started flipping through AM radio channels loaded with various songs filled with simple but meaningful stories and music.

Following one of those songs, the disc jockey (host) welcomed his regular guest doctor to answer phone-in questions from callers.

I paused my channel surfing, and that's when I met Dr. Ulyses Stuckum for the first time.

The caller must have been "a regular" more interested in cornering Dr. Stuckum than exchanging medical information.

The caller asked, "Dr Stuckum, I've got a serious problem. Lately, I've only been able to satisfy my wife five times a night. What's my problem, doctor?"

I won't lie. I snorted laughter at the idiotic question and wondered how the doctor would respond. There was a slight pause, and then Dr. Stuckum responded.

"I'm so glad you called in. Here's your problem."

Breathless, I waited to hear Stuckum's deduction on the matter.

"You're a liar." Then Dr Stuckum hung up on the caller and said, "Next!"

I guffawed. Tears of laughter rolled down my cheeks. I knew then that I had found a West Texas Medical communication genius willing to play and use humor.

Over the years, Dr. Stuckum and I have become very close friends, and he never fails to put a twist on words and concepts that are unexpected and funny while being insightful.

So, when my producer and I talked about the third book in my "Now that makes me mad ...about——" series ("**Now that makes me mad ...about men!**"; and "**Now that makes me mad ...in the bedroom!**"), I just had to involve Dr. Ulyses Stuckum.

I tend to be straightforward, but I believe Dr. Stuckum will make you think... and maybe even laugh. In his publicity photos, Stuckum is always holding a brain, so he's often called "The Doctor with two brains." You're going to like this guy.

Chapter Six

"The Current State of Politics"

Chapter 2

"The Current State of Politics"

Trying to give the *Current State of Politics* in the United States is like trying to nail *Jello* to a wall. About the time you think you have defined the problem, an explosion of stupidity happens, and you realize that things are much worse than you could have imagined. That's where we find ourselves right now.

America has survived the buffoonery of the current Liberal Democratic administration not because of its wisdom or effective leadership but because of America's long-standing strength and resilience. However, the Biden/Harris administration has pushed our country's financial indebtedness to a dangerous limit, and the crux of the problem begins at a single point.

"Special Interest Groups" or "Money Thugs"

The term *"Special Interest group"* is just too broad and soft of a term to describe the cancer that is gnawing away at the vital organs of America. The power of special interest groups and their financial stranglehold on the elected officials in our government (state and federal) is relentless.

More than One Master

The Bible tells us that no man can have more than one master. He's it! If there is more than one master, one is always favored over the other. Our country's politics is divided because of special interest groups with massive amounts of money they dole out to Congressmen, Congresswomen, and Senators (possibly presidents and their families) who control the spending of the funds drawn primarily from taxes.

A question about salaries

Since we pay our government's salaries from our people's taxes, we should have a serious interest in their finances. These are the salaries of the highest members of the Federal Government, Congressional Representatives, and the Executive Branch.

President $400,000
Vice President. $235,100*
Speaker of the House $223,500
House and Senate Majority & Minority Leaders/Senate
President Pro Tempore $193,400
House/Senate Members & Delegates. $174,000
Chief Justice, Supreme Court. $312,200
Associate Justices, Supreme Court. $298,500

Who is really in the White House?

What do we really know about the man in the White House? What do we know about the Vice President he chose to be his partner in all parts of the administration, including its deepest secrets?

WhenI asked www.Wikipedia.org, 'What was Joe Biden's GPA in college,' their response was: "… when he (Joe Biden) got a poor 1.9-grade point average for the semester, his parents told him that he had to give up football to concentrate on his classes. He continued to get mostly"C" and "D" grades for his next two semesters. His grades then began to improve, but never became especially good."

This information tells us that in college, Joe Biden was more interested in football than in studying. Has he changed?

In 1987 the *Associated Press* reported this:

"Sen.Joseph R. Biden Jr. claimed during a campaign appearance in New Hampshire last spring that he finished in the top half of his law school class, although records indicate he finished near the bottom," Newsweek magazine reported today."

Ina videotape released by the public service cable network C-SPAN, the DelawareDemocrat was asked at a campaign stop in Claremont, N.H., about what law schoolhe attended and how well he did.

"I went to(Syracuse) law school on a full academic scholarship," said Biden, who has beenbeset by revelations that he plagiarized in law school and used portions of aspeech by British Labor Party leader Neil Kinnock without credit.

On the tape, Biden says he "ended up in the top half" of his class. "I won the international moot court competition. . . . I was the outstanding student in the political science department (as an undergraduate). . . . I graduated with three degrees from college," Biden told the questioner.

'Higher IQ Than You'

A clearly angered Biden added: "I think I probably have a much higher IQ than you do."

Last week, however, the presidential candidate said at a news conference that he had finished 76th in a law school class of 85. Records he released indicated he had a partial, need-based scholarship and student loans.

The tape was aired April 12 as part of the network's "Road to the White House" series, C-SPAN spokeswoman Nan Gibson said.

News week magazine said Biden does not mention the moot-court competition on his resumeand did not win the political science award at University of Delaware, where he received a single B.A. in political science and history.

Biden told the New York Times that he was "frustrated" and "angry as hell" about the Newsweek report.

"It's so easy to make things look like there's something sinister about them," he said. "I guess every single word I've said is going to be dissected now."" (https://www.latimes.com/archives/la-xpm-198 7-09-21-mn-6104-story.html)

In thirty-seven years of public life since that 1987 AP story, Joe Biden's propensity to fabricate the truth has not changed, except possibly, it's gotten worse.

President Biden's 2022 net worth... in dollars

PolitiFact reported that "actor James Woods in December shared an image on X (formerly Twitter) claiming that Biden's net worth had increased from $9 million in 2019 to $41 million in 2022. In actuality, "Middle-Class Joe" has a net worth (we think) at $10 million."

We don't actually know how much money "middle-class Joe" has now because that info is hidden. But, if you happen to be a Republican candidate opposing Biden's/Harris re-election, then everything is open record.

As a point of comparison, according to Google.com, "When President Obama entered the White House, he had a net worth of $1.3 million, and a 2017 report by *American University* speculated that he could earn as much as $242.5 million in post-White House income.

It's surprising how $400,000/year can grow to $242.5 million in just eight years of being president.

The importance of having a Foundation (not a place to stash cash)

After many weeks of bouncing off the walls of my tiny office on the first floor, my wife decided I should have a new office on the second floor. So, knowing who holds the most power in my home, I moved my operation upstairs. It was a big office, and I finally had room to spread things out. Additionally, big windows on the second floor allowed me a better view of the new subdivision behind us.

I watched one of the homes get its new foundation, and it awakened memories about how we need to examine the foundation of politics in America.

Almost overnight, the workers built the forms and laid out the foundation tendons. The next day, the cement truck poured the new foundation. In just 72 hours, I watched the carpenters begin to build on the uncured foundation. It's for sure that only a piece of skin had started to set. But that didn't stop the carpenters.

My father's words once again rose from the deeper areas of my brain, and I recalled one of our moments together. Dad said, "Son, you have to create a sturdy foundation before building the penthouse on top. "It seemed pretty obvious, but many years later, I still see people building the upper floors and not paying serious attention to preserving the foundation that will carry the weight of the new structure... in construction or life.

What a concept: "Build a foundation before we build the penthouse." From a construction standpoint, Dad was right on target. But as we look at America and its struggle to remain the 'shining beacon on the hill,' it would help us remember Dad's words of wisdom and focus on the foundation of our country. Everybody wants a penthouse, but many only get an outhouse, and there's no longer a Sears Catalogue to provide the final paperwork.

Some seriously brilliant American founders

Many years ago, the founders of our great nation were a fiercely dedicated group of brilliant pre-Americans. They didn't have AI, computers, or even a *BigChief tablet* with a pencil the size of a horse's hind leg. Yet, they undertook drawing the documents on which to build our nation. They focused intently on the primary objective of forming this new country. "Freedom" was the central concept (The Foundation) that all the forming fathers agreed they wanted in America. Without ***Freedom,*** *t*hey could stay with England and save much more tea.

Today, "freedom" remains the central point we must focus on to keep America alive. Many say we build the penthouse when we have problems agreeing on the foundation. Face it: We must focus on our foundation, or the penthouses we build will crumble. Even today, Republicans often forget to focus on the foundation and gladly participate in eating the members of our own party. This must stop!

Strategy Note to my Republican House Members

How many times do you have to replace a House of Representatives Speaker held hostage to the power of a single individual or small group of power-hungry Congressional Representatives to realize that this Congressional Speaker 'replacement game' has some pretty big consequences? **Republicans...how about using a democrat tact ic...stick together on key issues, or the public perceives you to be very weak and disorganized. The perception of weakness invites attack by Democrats and special interest, well-funded vultures. Focus...**

The Definition of Freedom

Different people define "Freedom" differently, but without agreement on a single definition, all else is meaningless.

Keith Robinson 1966 as Ben Franklin

As a high school boy, I had the opportunity to play the character Benjamin Franklin in a stage performance. (Yep, that's me in high school.) In preparation for my performance, I went into the library and read many books on Benjamin Franklin. What a remarkable man! Although somewhat "frisky" as well, he was dedicated to the concept of freedom that was born into this new country of America.

Although I can't remember what I put in my coffee this morning, I do remember one of the lines I was giving the audience, captured in this photo.

"I wonder if the people that are born into America will realize the gift that they've been given out right in the crib ...for nothing? Will they know that if you are not free, you are, sir, lost without hope? Freedom is precious, and I have but one question: would you be willing to die for freedom?"

That's commitment. Unfortunately, but truthfully, very few in politics have the level of commitment borne by our forefathers. One person who stands out in my mind is Senator John Kennedy. He can whip up on someone, and they will still love him.

How can you spot an infant?

As a young doctoral student, I recall the psychiatrist teaching our class, and he defined the primary characteristics of "infants." He said, "I want what I want...when I want it." The infant demands instant gratification of their wants and a willingness to ignore the life-giving "needs." It is a childish expectation.

Today, I watch Liberal Democrats, led by Senator Schumer, pitching "chum" into the barrel of insatiable piranha, wanting trillions of dollars that America doesn't have. The Omnibus bill recently proposed and passed is so packed with pork that it makes pigs ashamed. "I want what I want...when I want it."

We've agreed it's a childish expectation, but Democrats vote on these bills as though they never have to pay for the privileges they get or "take" because of the majority they hold. America goes trillions deeper in debt each time the omnibus pork pit is voted on. Our children, grandchildren, and great-grandchildren will pay for this debt in many ways.

Booker T. Washington was a great American and spoke wisdom we should never forget.

A lie doesn't become truth,
Wrong doesn't become right,
And evil doesn't become good,
Just because it's accepted by a majority.
Booker T. Washington

Chapter Seven

"The Current State of Politics" (SPLIT)

We need "wisdom," and that's often very hard to find.

God blessed me far more than I deserve regarding a wonderful set of parents. Mom and Dad were unquestionably dedicated to each other in love and matrimony, and they used country logic to form the wisdom of parenting. Their photos are in the dedication of the book.

When mom became pregnant, and it was time to deliver the surprise packagef rom God…, the doctor told my mom, "Don't have another one because this one is going to be a handful." Clairvoyant doctors are hard to find these days.

Dad was a man of "integrity" and "wisdom." If Dad said it, you could bet your last dollar that it was "true." It shouldn't be surprising how "integrity" and "wisdom" go hand in hand. If there is a void of "integrity" in the person, "wisdom" will most likely not exist either.

Dad could' think outside the box,' a cliché used far too often, but it was true his entire life. And he loved me with a love that could move mountains. Sometimes, our children are those mountains.

Dad and I worked together to put a roof on our tiny home in Midwest City, Oklahoma. One of those pesky hailstorms that frequented Oklahoma demanded a new roof be installed on our house. Life lessons abounded as we rolled out the tarpaper on the decking and nailed it to place, and together, we carried bundles of shingles onto the roof. Those are heavy. We reached a point where we nailed the shingles, one by one, when we ran out of nails. Dad asked if I could go to the hardware store and buy enough nails for us to finish the job. Back in 1953, $ 20 dollars could buy a lot of nails. I watched my father take the only $20-dollar bill in his pocket and give it to me, saying, "Just bring back the change that Fred (the store owner) gives you.

Our family lacked a lot of money, so every penny was important. I put the money in my pocket, descended the ladder, and headed for Fred's hardware. The day was beautiful, and the hardware store was not far away.

Tragedy can still happen on a beautiful day, and on that day, it happened. The $20-dollar bill was not in my pocket when I arrived at the hardware store. In tears of disappointment flowing from my eyes, Fred gave me the roofing tacks, but I had to tell my dad I had lost the money. The return trip to our house seemed like 500 miles.

When I arrived home with tears still streaming, Dad came down off the roof, and we sat on the ground under a shade tree with his arms wrapped around me. "You want to tell me about these tears?"

"I don't know how it happened, but...I lost the money. It must have fallen out of my pocket." Dad pulled me close to his chest, and wrapped his arms around me. I felt love fill my broken heart."

"Son, people make mistakes; the important thing is that we learn the lesson that always comes with every mistake." Today, you made a $20 mistake but learned a lesson worth far more than the money."

When I graduated from Drake University and was on my way to professional school, Dad and I had a life-changing talk about *real wisdom* and evil." His brief explanation of "Real Wisdom" is captured below. I pray our Senators, congressmen/Congresswomen, and presidents use real wisdom as they lead our country, for it feels like Evil is all around.

Illusive Real Wisdom

Son, evil is slippery and will try to divide good people by using the power of "doubt." You will often be fooled if you look for wisdom and think you can identify it by the color of someone's skin or the number of degrees behind someone's name. Don't look for perfection in people. Look for the wisdom in someone's heart and willingness to do good for others. There, you just might find someone who knows real wisdom.

Bennie J. Robinson (my father...now in heaven)

Commitment to building the sturdy foundation of being an American is something people take far too lightly. Many people think that America will always be here, but we need to wake up because right now, there are forces in America...evil forces, who are trying to destroy its foundation. If they destroy the foundation of America, it will fall, and the shining beacon on the hill will disappear. So, we must preserve the foundation of America to continue enjoying the freedom of being an American. I know it sounds corny, but it's true.

How do we teach our children about the American Foundation?

How do we focus on building a foundation and making it stronger to handle other aspects of America that people are trying to build? It's a word that many people don't like. It's "sacrifice" or, in other words, "I don't get what I want "when" I want it, but when I can afford it, and it's the right thing to do ...at this point in our development. Just because we can pass a law to do something doesn't mean we should do that. There is a trite but true statement: People love sausage but don't want to see how it's made. They don't want to know what's in some hotdogs. Trust me, in some instances, it's disgusting.

A pathology professor once said, "Do you know the things that can fall into an industrial sausage machine?" By the end of the lecture, nobody ever wanted sausage or hot dogs again. Yet, Americans consume 7 billion hot dogs between *Memorial Day and Labor Day each year, according to the National Hot Dog and Sausage Council*.

What goes on in the backrooms of Congress would make many thriller novels appear boring. Being in Congress today is nothing short of a blood sport. It's not for timid or squeamish people. If you get elected to Congress, wear your body armor. You'll need it.

What's in a name?

Not long ago the www.huffpost.com ran an article about *very unique business names*. (I am not an owner of any of these businesses or even involved in their industries, except for visiting some of them out of curiosity).

(https://www.huffpost.com/entry/the-25-most-ridiculous-busine ss-names-ever_b_5924663ae4b0b28a33f62fd9) These are actual business names used to attract positive attention in the public.

1.   *"Goin'Postal* I still remember when at least 14 people were gunned down in a post office in Edmond, Oklahoma. A somewhat negative beginning for the term Going Postal. But now, they are turning that around negative into a positive with over 200 locations across the US. What makes me worried is that I was born not far from Edmond and am writing a book titled "Now that makes me mad..."

2.   *Kum and Go.* I won't comment on this branding job done by their corporate office. They have 400 stores, so I guess the name worked.

3.   *Passmore Gas & Propane.* Maybe this is the reason Biden is against the Oil and Gas industry. Who knows? But when gas reaches $145/gallon and the EV charging stations fail, somebody had better figure out if rebranding might be needed. I can see it now: "Biden Gas and EV." You might as well buy it there because once you pay the bill for your fill-up, you won't be able to go anywhere.

4.   *Amigone Funeral Home*: This is a classic name...for those who aren't really sure.

5.   *Chew-N-Butts:* Believe it or not, a tobacco shop is named this. Butt...this one should be dedicated to the White House aides who are learning to deal with geriatric screaming fits because of low-to-negative polling numbers.

Names indicate a little history of the family that has worn that name. Names always show up on tax rolls and tombstones. As I look at many of our politicians, I wonder if history will be kind to their memory once they are deceased.

Years ago, I taught a class on *"Creative ways of dealing with Fear and Anger."* I asked the class members to write their own obituary. When they read out loud what they wrote, most admitted that the wordsthey wrote were what they wanted people to remember… not actually how theylived.

Remembering"O.J."

Today, O.J. Simpson died. Now, there's a name that will be remembered more than "O. J." being the short version of "orange juice." Will he be remembered for the many good things he did or because of being prosecuted for the tragic deaths of his wife, Nicole, and Ron Goldman? Names tie us to families or events from our past. President Biden announced that he sent his condolences to O.J.'s family because of his death. But they failed to mention condolences for the deaths of Nicole Simpson and Ron Goldman. Where is the wisdom here?

We want wisdom, now.

To understand the current state of politics in America, we must look back at the foundation on which it was formed because what's true is this: we don't know, and most of us are unwilling to wait for whatever we want. We want everything now.

I have a good friend in California who is also a chaplain. He once told me of the "Prayer for Patience" mentioned by a younger police officer he was serving. Here it is: "Lord, give me patience…and give it to me NOW."

As I write those words, I realize I am too impatient, like most of you.For example, the microwave takes far too long to spin for one slow, never-ending minute. It seems like an eternity. Nine months for a baby to be born, we want to know <u>now</u> if the baby is a boy or a girl. Nobody wants a yellow-colored baby bedroom. So, we peek to satisfy the need for immediate answers to what we want. Our desire for immediate gratification cannot be denied most of the time.

Some Senators and Congressional representatives use the need for immediate answers and make immediate laws to solve difficult problems in America. Laws can't change morals or ethics in humans. Some people must make mistakes to learn the lesson. If they refuse to learn from the mistake in their judgment, they must wait for maturity to catch up with the responsibilities needed in the leadership job. That applies to The President as well.

The most significant purpose of American politics is Mutual Protection.

What do you do with a country filled with 'free Americans' surrounded by powerful forces and people who want to take away their freedom and enslave them? You protect them from as much of the enslaving powers as possible. On that point, we realize that Americans become stronger as we defend our freedom. Nobody wants a totalitarian country where cameras are everywhere to spy on us Americans. Just a minute, that's what we have right now. Without meaning to awaken paranoia, but that's happening now. AI is watching through the eye of the camera.

We are not trying to 'protect freedom' but to regain it. Regaining freedom is much more complicated than fighting to keep it. Ink in the water is really hard to remove. Prevention is still the best answer.

The initial purpose of America was to band people together for <u>mutual protection </u>from those who tried to destroy its foundation.

That purpose continues to be the most significant responsibility for those who love America because there are many powerful countries and twisted super-wealthy people within our own country who would jump for joy if America failed.

American Borders...you knew this topic was coming.

The introduction of this book included a political cartoon that goes straight to the subject's heart. For America to remain America, we must have well-defined borders that selectively admit those who are dedicated to perpetuating America and not destroying it. The system currently in place because of the Presidential mandate allows everyone, including those who want to destroy America, to come in and begin that process.

These people who break into our country as their first official act claim to be in search of "The American Dream." Every night, the news media displays those same people demanding instantaneous "rights." They are seen on the news demanding that the country they left behind to come to America is what they want here. They fly the flags of the country they left. They teach others how to break our laws and become squatters, destroying the property rights of others and stealing the value of someone else's home. They beat our police officers and bring drugs to America that will kill millions. of Americans, and now they yell *Death to America*. In my humble opinion, these people need to go home today.

Not all who come over the southern border or northern borders of America want to destroy this great country. Still, when you're dealing with 13 million *unknowns*, many of whom have come from the jails, mental institutions, and violent gangs of many countries across this world, *to be wise, we must hope for the best but to survive we must prepare for the worst.* We must admit that a 'Pollyanna approach' to homeland security is inviting someone to commit a 911 event somewhere in America. With no close examination of these migrants/illegals/aliens, there is no primary dedication to the perpetuation of America for our children.

When you live in an "instantaneous society," everything moves far too fast—often too fast. It's much easier for younger generations to move too fast, and it's difficult to get them to slow down. Long-lasting relationships take time to develop, even when it is your relationship with America.

13+Million American Guests (aliens, migrants, and got-aways)

It surprises me how many relatively younger people lack any concern for the 13+ million unwanted and uninvited migrants and 'gotaways' crossing into our country illegally. The fact that President Biden and Kamala will not stop the migrants from entering does not mean that it's legal. It just means that the President and the Democrat party is willing to ignore the law for some reason. The apparent drain on the fixed overhead American expenses to help these folks who cannot legally get a job should set each of us on our heels, asking, "What the heck are you doing, Mr. President?" Madame VP, are you ever going to try to help save America? This is not a laughing matter. I think we know.

However, insulated from direct contact or anyone else's account-ability, the President does it anyway. Does he want 13 million new Americans on the books? If we can't afford the expenses of feeding, housing, and medical care for the Americans already here, the home-less veterans who put their lives on the line for this country, and the

American elderly who barely survive on dribbles of Medicare/Medicaid/Social Security, then why let all these unknowns in? How about older people who live on beans and rice because Congress has robbed money from the Social Security System and replaced that money with worthless IOUs that will never be repaid?

Will these aliens be good citizens or just numbers on the books that will **change the number of people living in a geographic area? The US Census looks at the total number of people in a geographic area, not whether they are legal citizens. That changes representation in Congress, which changes votes. There's the reason for Liberal Democrats pushing open borders.**

Americans believe in "Legal Immigration" but not "open borders."

What happens to all the immigrants who have stood in line, studied the Bill of Rights and the Constitution, and passed a test on knowing this country before being admitted into it as an American Citizen? By allowing the tsunami of people to breach the border, the President has kicked dirt in the faces of American immigrants who respected our process for becoming citizens. Most of the time, you'll find these are very different immigrants than those who break their way into America. When breaking the law is their first official act in America, how can they claim to be worthy of the fruits of American citizenship?

Whatever you want...pay the price, and we're not talking about money.

I believe it was Napoleon Hill who said, "Whatsoever you want, oh discontented man (woman), step up, pay the price, and take it." Being given freedom in a country where you paid no price for admission is a setup for the failure of that dream.

I truly believe that God had his hand on America and its founding fathers when this country was born; his hand remains on America today.

Freedom of Religion **is a right, but our laws were founded on Judeo-Christian principles.**

America was formed on Judeo-Christian principles, but that does not mean that everyone has to be a Christian, a Jew, or a specific religion to be a good American citizen and live in this country. The founding fathers recognized the Judeo-Christian principles, and God put them into place to show us how to relate to Him. "Freedom" comes from God, not from manmade laws. Folks get mixed up about that.

The 10 Commandments...don't skip over this

When you look at the 10 Commandments, you look at the basic instructions needed to be a human, which should be in every American. And those basic instructions found in the 10 Commandments became the foundation of America. We are a country where people individually define how they relate to God. Still, God helps us by giving us the 10 Commandments as a tool to relate to Him and the perpetuation of America. So, these rules (commandments) are vital, and those who come into America and peel away the basic rules needed for this country to remain alive are not worthy of being Americans. They're not even a visitor. (They are an intruder, no matter how AOC tries to twist that truth.)

Again, these are my opinions, but I had better let Dr. Stuckum give us his thoughts.

Dr. Keith A. Robinson

Chapter Eight

Almost Political News (SPLIT)

Commentary by Dr. Ulyses Stuckum

"Almost Political News"

Mass Skunk Airlift Proposal to Deter Illegal Border Crossings... Backfires

For Immediate Release

In a desperate attempt to deter illegal border crossings, border states are exploring an unconventional solution: deploying a squadron of 500 angry skunks via airlift over the southern border.

Frustrated by razor wire's inefficacy, a petulant, myopic federal bureaucracy, and traditional border security measures, Texas officials are brainstorming creative ways to send a strong message to would-be border crossers. The proposed plan involves gathering 500 deranged skunks from skunk rescue centers across the country and airlifting them using giant nets over the border. The hope is that the skunks' pungent aroma and aggressive demeanor will serve as a non-lethal deterrent, urging border crossers to reconsider their decision and return home.

"It's a simple, one-time application," says Governor Greg Abbott of Texas, one of the leading proponents of the plan." Just one whiff of those crazy skunks, and I guarantee they'll think twice about crossing our Texas border illegally."

The skunk airlift is set to end at a tiny airstrip on the outskirts of the sanctuary capital city of Sacramento, California. Governor Gavin Newsome's office has been advised of the airlift but didn't respond. Support staff for Governor Newsome was away measuring the White House Oval Office for drapes and was unavailable for comment.

Because of the overwhelming stench of liberalism in Sacramento, Abbott believes that the toxic skunk aroma will be barely noticed. On a positive note, it is believed that the deranged skunks each immediately will be granted asylum under *California Wild Animal Sanctuary laws*, given free veterinary healthcare for life, and be provided lifetime birth control treatments paid for by the remaining California inhabitants. Additionally, the patriotic skunks will receive a bucket of dead mice, deceased pet moles, rats, birds, and their eggs, sterilized highway roadkill carcasses, endangered grasshoppers, tamed wasps, soured honeybees, terminally disabled crickets, migratory beetles and their larvae, and all of the fresh fruit they can eat from the beautiful California orchards...every month. California liberal research shows that these migrant skunks will be immediately eligible for a monthly debit card with $20,000 free to spend from the Dwindling TaxFunding accounts periodically drained by Governor Newsome and California liberals on stupid projects that are driving high-paying workers and their families to move toward Texas, a thriving state with no income taxes, to save what little they have left in the bank while they can.

However, some critics worry about the unintended ***consequences of such a plan. This is where the Stinky Border Flyover Mission*** may backfire.

"Sure, it might deter illegal border crossings, but what about the innocent bystanders caught in the skunks' line of fire," questions skunk immigration rights activist Maria Rodriguez. "We just can't subject people to that kind of olfactory assault."

Others point out the logistical challenges of coordinating a skunk airlift of such magnitude, including concerns about the skunks' welfare during transit and the potential for mid-air skirmishes among the disgruntled passengers. "We are prepared for little things like this," said Cessna 182, thriller pilot, flight instructor, and flight team coordinator for the ***Stinky Border Flyover Mission*** (SBFM).

"This ***Stinky Border Flyover Mission***(a.k.a. skunk transport border flyover) is more than fragrant folly; it takes some serious tactical planning to pull off something like this. We have amassed a volunteer squadron of 25 Cessna 182 pilots with their planes. Engineers from NASA have donated the nets previously used to capture the returning space capsules from the water landings. With a bit of reinforcement to ensure we don't lose any furry passengers, we're ready to go. Texas border farmers and ranchers have donated $1,000,000 for the fuel of the entire squadron of pilots. Former President Donald Trump has donated $1,000,000 to cover other flight expenses. Lt. Governor Dan Patrick will fly in the lead plane for incidental decisions and live news interviews.

At just the right moment, the Lt. Governor will signal to release 10,000 Red MAGAhats as the squadron crosses into California airspace. ***Fox News*** has agreed to provide news coverage on the event for international distribution throughout its network. NBC, CBS, and other liberal news media were invited to participate. Unfortunately, the only seats left in the Cessna's for news reporters from those networks were in the tail-end plane, rigged with an advanced air filtering technology designed for use by the pilot only. They have declined coverage of this event, believing it would leave a negative atmosphere for other Democrats running for office.

The entire cast from ***The View,*** along with Congressman A. Schiff, Senator Schumer, and Congresswoman AOC, were invited to ride in the nets with the deranged skunks...but the skunks voted that down.

Just to be safe, the owners of the deranged skunks have all signed "legal parental permission documents" to transport their fuzzy, fragrant pets so that there can be no claim of transporting stinky pets across state lines without permission. According to prosecutor Fani, "Kidnapping pet skunks" is a little-known Federal offense, but still somewhat of a severe claim...and I knew that Trump was behind it someway. "So, we must protect our team during this aerial public service mission because we all know some brainless prosecutor who wants to "Bragg" about one more frivolous 'trumped up claim' would try to cause trouble. So, we're legally covered with the documents safely secured in President Biden's garage beside his unused auto and multiple boxes of Top Secret documents illegally taken over years of being in public service.

"There are only two real potential challenges we're still working on," said the Lead pilot for project **SBFM**. "First, we decided on a wing formation flight as none of the pilots wanted to fly their planes behind all the fragrant payloads. And second, it will be necessary to land to refuel and reach our final destination near Sacramento." A group of resourceful retired Airborne Rangers led by Ranger Diebold have created glide parachutes that lift the nets full of our passengers off the ground. Still, it can be bumpy during take-off and landing, dragging behind the Cessna's. One of the Airborne Rangers, a rather inventive soul, has created an undercarriage slide that will help. This will keep these little black and white passengers friendly and safe during the ride. Tactically, at just the right moment during the border flyover, the pilots will simultaneously fly their planes upside down to invert the enclosed net holding the skunks. This surprise inversion should raise the anxiety in the deranged skunks (and possibly a few pilots) just enough to initiate the fragrant release of a massive plume of stinky, sticky toxins covering the border razor wire and serving as a deterrent for at least six months. It will also help us find the got-aways.

It's a great plan! Once the netted passengers are fragrantly empty and moderately composed, the squadron of Cessna's, with trailing nets, will set a course for California. Destination: the outskirts of Sacramento, where a tiny landing strip was once used for state-approved marijuana drug trafficker deliveries. By then, the skunks should be refueled for their release in sunny California. They will have worked hard to provide vital border security for America that the Biden/Harris/Democrat administration didn't even consider. Yep, it's time for these patriotic pets to enjoy the "pet vacation" of their lifetimes.

Despite the skepticism, proponents of the plan remain undeterred, citing the need for bold, innovative solutions to address the ongoing border crisis created by President Biden, Border Czar Kamala Harris, and Congressional Liberal Democrats."

"We're thinking outside the box here," asserts Governor Abbott. "Sometimes, you need a little stink to get your point across." As the debate fumes, one thing is clear: the ***Stinky Border Flyover Mission*** proposal has sparked a lively conversation about the intersection of US border security, animal welfare, and unconventional tactics in the ongoing battle against illegal immigration.

One final note: Florida Governor Ron DeSantis has also expressed curiosity about a possible waterfront border security flyover.

(**Note:** No skunks were hurt or emotionally traumatized during the writing of this story)

(Written only in jest!)

Chapter Nine

"Wrong People...wrong jobs!"

Chapter 3

"Wrong People...Wrong Jobs!"

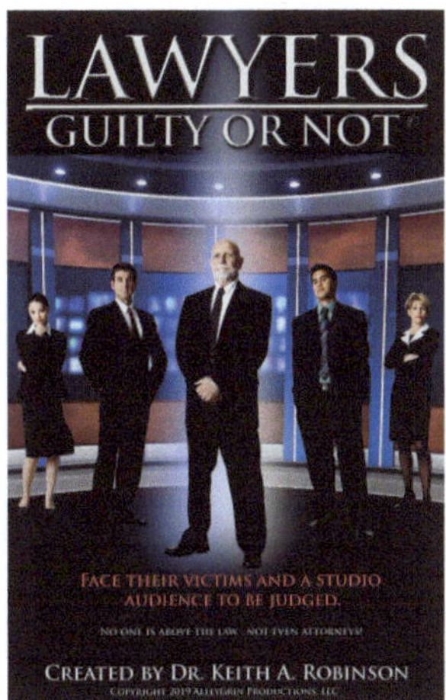

Discernment" is an interesting word that is not used in everyday talk but probably should be used more. When you look up the formal definition of the word in the Merriam-Webster dictionary, this is what you'll find: "the quality of being able to and comprehend what is ." Within that definition are two key 'power words' that give understanding to that definition. Those two words are "grasp" and "obscure." "Grasp" means "to take or seize eagerly." "Obscure" means "shrouded in or hidden by darkness."

The gift of "discernment" requires that the person be able to grasp a concept or event that is shrouded in or hidden by darkness. Hold that definition in your mind briefly while we talk about wolves.

Understanding Wolves

During my years as a biology and comparative anatomy student, it became important to understand a creature's anatomy and what instinctively motivates it as it lives.

Wolves are an interesting species. Merriam-Webster dictionary defines them this way: "any of several large predatory canids (genus

Canis) that are active mostly at night, live and hunt in packs, and resemble the related dogs." Then it adds the reference to some of us humans who survive as wolves:" a fierce, rapacious ("living on prey") or destructive person." Now, there's an interesting jump between species.

Lawyers, Guilty or Not

In 2019, my work as a screenwriter pushed me to think outside the box for interesting ways to reverse roles and turn those situations into a movie or TV show that would capture an audience. ***Lawyers, Guilty or Not***, (copyright 2019 AlleyGrin Productions) was the result. The poster for that show captured the essence of the action that would happen as lawyers got to be judged by an audience of those on whom the lawyers had prayed (and not in a religious way).

The Two Wolves – a Cherokee story

Growing up in Oklahoma, you learn a lot by living amidst Indian culture. In its own unique way, the Cherokee story of the two wolves is a perfect example of how the wisdom of animal behavior can relate to human nature. The story teaches us that two wolves are inside each of us, one representing good and the other representing evil. Whichever wolf you feed will determine which one grows stronger and dominates your actions.

This is a powerful lesson that can help us understand our own behavior and the behavior of those around us. On the other hand, we can also learn negative things about humans by observing the behavior of animals, such as the destructive and rapacious nature of wolves. It is important to use discernment and observe these behaviors without judgment to understand better and navigate our complex world.

Here is the ***Two Wolves Story.*** This story will stick with you and is worthy of being shared with children.

THE TWO WOLVES

A CHEROKEE STORY

A young boy came to his Grandfather, filled with anger at another boy who had done him an injustice. The old Grandfather said to his grandson, "Let me tell you a story. I, too, at times, have felt a great hate for those who have taken so much, with no sorrow for what they do. But hate wears you down, and hate does not hurt your enemy. Hate is like taking poison and wishing your enemy would die. I have struggled with these feelings many times."

"It is as if there are two wolves inside me; one wolf is good and does no harm. He lives in harmony with all around him and does not take offense when no offense was intended. He will only fight when it is right to do so and in the right way. But the other wolf, is full of anger. The littlest thing will set him into a fit of temper."

"He fights everyone, all the time, for no reason. He cannot think because his anger and hate are so great. It is helpless anger, because his anger will change nothing. Sometimes it is hard to live with these two wolves inside me, because both of the wolves try to dominate my spirit."

The boy looked intently into his grandfather's eyes and asked, "Which wolf will win, Grandfather?"

The Grandfather smiled and said, "The one I feed."

Social breakdown is happening across America

I may be showing signs of my age, but I am of the firm opinion that our society is showing some very negative signs of social breakdown. Recently, it seems like the normalcy of periodic feelings of anger at the actions of Democrats as a group has changed. Now, I scratch my head daily and think, 'What the heck is going on? Have large quantities of those illegal drugs daily coming across the open borders somehow found their way into the water supply of the Democrat Party?' The inner spirit of America is becoming twisted into an unrecognizable form.

The gene for hate seems to be growing rampant, especially among Liberal Democrats. For a long time, talk show hosts have kidded their audiences with the term **"Trump Derangement Syndrome."** Michael Savage is a conservative talk show host who coined the phrase "Liberalism is a Mental Disorder" and shared it with ten million weekly listeners through his massive, worldwide media footprint. When I first heard Savage use that phrase, I laughed. Now, with the Trump Derangement Syndrome used widely by Americans, there may be something to Savage's creativity.

Time to recognize a few people who may be the Wrong People...in the wrong job.

Nothing good can happen when you find yourself with the wrong person holding a position for which they appear to be a non-match. If you don't recognize the mistake of putting that person in a position in which they are unprepared to accomplish the tasks that go with it, a train wreck will soon happen. Chaos will occur, and bedlam will result. But we keep believing the bull, and folks keep electing Liberal Democrats who have an almost "disdain for the job they are seeking" based on DEI, skin color, or sexual orientation. These things don't help us identify the right person for the right job. Democrats seem quite adept at putting people who are absolutely the wrong person in the wrong jobs. Then they wonder why things don't get fixed when they are broken. Time for a change in thinking.

I have selected a few people from our "political soup of characters" whom I believe are the wrong people for the political jobs they hold. Wikipedia has provided their background, but it has been edited slightly for emphasis.

April 17, 2024, a day that will live in infamy as one of the darkest days for the US Congress.

Alejandro May-orkas -Secretary of Homeland Securi-ty

Wikipedia has this to say about **Alejandro Nicolas Mayorkas,** (born November 24, 1959). "Myorkas is an American lawyer and politician serving since 2021 as the seventh United States Secretary of Homeland Security. During the Obama Administration, he also served in the (DHS), first as director of United States Citizenship and Immigration Service (2009–2013), and as Deputy Secretary of DHS (2013–2016).

Mayorkas was born in Havana, Cuba. Shortly after the Cuban Revolution , his family fled to Florida and later settled in California. He graduated from UC Berkley in history with honors and subsequently earned his J.D. from Loyola Marymount University. After law school, Mayorkas worked as an Assistant United States Attorney and was appointed the United States attorney for the Central District of California in Los Angeles during the administrations of President Bill Clinton and George W Bush, where he oversaw the prosecution of high-profile criminal cases.

Mayorkas is not a stupid man but is a man who has learned to hunt with a pack of Democrat wolves who protect his frequent choice to lie in front of Congress, camera interviews, and any time he needs to cover his backside for the bad choices he has made. For these stellar acts of defiant lying, he has been Impeached by the House of Representatives. His repeated actions of untruth and failure to follow the laws of the United States have brought him a place in the history of our country, that will never be forgotten. Those are the facts. By the way, he swore an oath to uphold the laws of the United States. There is a disconnect somewhere.

Mayorkas has learned that he can break the laws he swore to uphold because he knows that the other wolves in the pack will shred the US Constitution and the laws enacted by Congress, flooding our homeland with 11-13 million illegals, 513,100+ Illegal Immigrant apprehensions, 43,700+ criminal arrests (so far), 38,400+ felony charges, and 488 Million+ lethal doses of Fentanyl seized at his 'closed and secure' border.

Mayorkas is in the pack. The pack protects him, and, in my opinion, he has singlehandedly victimized every illegal man, woman, and child he allowed into this country. He has become a co-conspirator worthy of being pictured along with others who have committed treason against each man, woman, and American child in this country.

What I don't think he yet knows is that when wolves choose, they attack another wolf within the pack and tear it to shreds. The hunter becomes the hunted by their own pack.

Because of what we have observed collectively since the day he was appointed and confirmed by Congress, Mayorkas has faced Congress and the people of the United States and lied about our homeland security. For that reason, **Alejandro N. Mayorkas** is now the namesake of the coveted ***Mayorkian Red Hand Award***. When this man swears to tell the truth, the whole truth and nothing but the truth...it's pretty safe to say...he's lying. **Wrong Person...Wrong Job!**

Congressman Eric Swallwell

Wikipedia provides background on **Representative Eric Swalwell** (born November 16, 1980) is an American lawyer and politician serving as the for since 2023. His district, numbered as the US Representative from 2013 to 2023, covers most of eastern Alameda County and part of central Contra Costa County. . He is a member of the Democratic Party.

Born in Sac City, Iowa, Swalwell spent his childhood in Dublin, California. He was a First Generation College Student, having briefly attended Campbell University on a soccer scholarship before earning degrees from the University of Maryland, College Park, and the University of Maryland, Baltimore. As a college student, Swalwell served as a student liaison to the College Park City Council and interned for Ellen Tauscher .

After college, Swalwell returned to California and worked as a deputy district attorney in Alameda County. He was appointed to multiple municipal commissions in Dublin and later served two years on the Dublin City Council. He was elected to the U.S. House of Representatives in 2012, defeating 40-year incumbent Pete Stark in an upset.

Swalwell has co-chaired the House Democratic Steering Committee since 2017. He was a candidate in the 2020 House Democratic Party presidential primaries from April to July 2019 before dropping out and endorsing Joe Biden. As of October 2021, Swalwell had voted in line with Joe Biden's stated position 100% of the time."

Even though Swalwell's past includes Midwestern Iowa values, he has learned to hunt with the pack of Democratic wolves to survive. I'm not sure he has learned that if you hang around with someone named "Fang," there's a good chance you'll get bit, and the poison may be slow-acting, but it tastes a lot like Kung Pao Chicken.

Wrong person...Wrong Job!

Chapter Ten

"Wrong People...wrong jobs!" (SPLIT)

Representative Nancy Pelosi

Voters don't know what to do without Nancy, but things seem to be much better without her 'hogwash' always in the media when serving as House Speaker.

Nancy has always been a sparkplug in government but the only thing that seems to work in Democrat Pelosi is her mouth. Ever since Republicans recovered "the People's House," necessitating her to give up the gavel of control, the House has had great direction, with Democrats only serving as boat anchors to slow down actual leadership of the people's business.

Unfortunately, Nancy Pelosi and her shark-like bite on the control of politics will be remembered for her famous (infamous), misguided, narcissistic political control. Someday, when she resigns from Congress, she will receive a congratulatory plaque that reads, ***I guess you'll have to vote on the bill in order to see what is in the bill***. With Nancy not in control of the House, it's for sure that the Representative's lunchroom expenses for ketchup, dill pickles, and other condiments will be on the rise. As an infant, Nancy was weaned on dill pickles rather than a pacifier, which greatly explains her outlook on life. As far as her success in representing her constituents, look at the California area she represents in the House. It's a shamble, too. <u>**Wrong Person...Wrong Job!**</u>

California Representative Adam Schiff

(Wikipedia) (Born June 22, 1960) Adam Schiff is an American lawyer, author, and politician serving as a US Representative from since 2001. A member of the Democrat Party, Schiff was a member of the California State Senate from 1996 to 2000.

Schiff graduated from Stanford and Harvard Law School. As an assistant United States attorney, he successfully prosecuted Soviet spy Richard Miller in 1993 and began running for office the following year. He represents California's 30th congressional district, which is centered in the Sam Gabroe; Valley east of Los Angeles.

Schiff chaired the House Intelligence Committee from 2019 to 2023 and was removed from it by Speaker Kevin McCarthy in 2023.

Wrong Person...Wrong Job!

George Santos

In an effort to be somewhat fair, I have to list a fallen star from the Republican ranks who might have gone far in the "World's biggest liars" competition. Because this book can only go about 200 pages and the Liberal Democrat Party is rather engorged with people who wear the damaged chromosome for truth, which needs to be removed from every cell in their bodies, I must mention Santos, where strong evidence shows it just might be true.

So, here are some of the fibs/potential misstatements of facts in the news regarding now-everyday citizen Santos. 1). At just 34 years of age, he has claimed to be a college volleyball star; 2) A pet philanthropist; 3) a high-rolling Wall Street investor; and 4) A Catholic from Brazil with Ukrainian and Jewish blood.

Democrats and Republicans pushed Santos out of Congress, which is a dubious distinction. This may have been the only thing Congress has truly agreed upon in a very long time.

George can be accurately described as 'a mixed breed' and was elected to office following Anthony Weiner. Go figure. Someone might want to hose down that office with some strong disinfectant to protect the next inhabitant.

The Republicans held their noses as long as possible and took away Santo's key to the Congressional toilet. They politely loaded all his claimed possessions into an old cardboard box once used by Joe Biden to load classified documents in his garage, escorted him to the Capital steps, and affixed a large piece of permanent duct tape to his mouth, forbidding him to ever repeat the words Republican...in perpetuity...throughout the Milky Way or its adjacent star systems.

I think A copy of the Ten Commandments might have been found in his almost empty office following his release from Congress. But Santo's version was missing: "Though shalt not lie." **Wrong perso n...wrong Job!**

Alexandria Ocasio-Cortez

(Wikipedia)

AOC was elected at 29 years of age to be the youngest woman ever to serve in Congress. Ms. AOC is living 96% proof that the brain doesn't complete development with full connection of neurons until much later in life. After graduating from Boston University *cum laude* she is said to have worked as an organizer for Bernie Sanders's presidential campaign. He lost.

With this background and education, AOC became a professional bartender in Manhattan and a high-paid waitress in a taqueria, fully utilizing her *Cum Laude* education from BU. A proud Democrat with a flair for grabbing the attention of any camera within five blocks of her immediate location (any location, any state, at any time of the day or night), AOC represents New York, District 114, which has taken on the appearance of a third world country, under the opinionated questionable leadership of this superliberal Democrat.

With her re-election potential in the negative numbers, many wonder what she will take on in the next phase of her young life, but they won't have to look very far.

"Maybe a Congressional Representative...Maybe an Actress"

It looks like every speech AOC makes might count as an acting performance for IMDB credits. Interestingly, AOC has listed herself as an "Actress, Writer, and Producer," but nowhere in this widely advertised document does she list her credentials as an esteemed **Con-**

gressional Representative. However, she did use the photo from her congressional elected position, but it looks like she considers herself **an actress**. I guess we should remember that each time she gets before a camera, which is...far too often. Enough said. **Wrong Person... Wrong Job!**

"One Law Per Person"

Congressman Bennie Thompson

(Wikipedia) Congressman Bennie G. Thompson is an elected member of the United States House of Representatives from Mississippi's 2ndCongressional District. Congressman Thompson claimed his seat in the House on April 20, 1993. He is a native of Bolton, Mississippi.

I had great hopes for Representative Bennie Thompson because he's not an attorney and shares his first name with my deceased father. But recently, he fell off the pedestal normally reserved for great statesmen when he introduced a bill aimed <u>only</u> at Former President Donald Trump.

We currently have almost 5,200 federal crime laws, many of which are never enforced in any way, but that didn't stop Rep. Bennie Thompson from filing one more potential law. I am told it will only affect former President Trump if it passes. It sounds like if President Trump died today, Rep. Bennie Thompson would only be happy if the body was dumped into a Liberal Democrat meat grinder and the Trump scraps were fed to pigs. This man appears to have deep-seated hate where there's supposed to be a heart for American's. **Wrong Person...Wrong Job!**

> **"You can fool some of the people all of the time,**
> **and all of the people some of the time,**
> **but you cannot fool all of the people all of the time."**
> **President Abe Lincoln**

In my opinion, there must be a way to identify these people who may have lost their "heart for service" to America and want to provide lip service to an ideology of hate or racism. I think these are the wrong people to represent the humans in our country. Hate will destroy us. In the past, **hate** primarily came from people or groups outside our country, but since President Biden and VP Kamala Harris have opened the southern border has been forcibly left open by Liberal Democrats, it's obvious that the hate has been invited and enabled to flourish. Now, I believe the biggest hate sources come from within our beloved country.

It is now more than obvious that what is growing is a former Presidential lynch mob. The attorney general of the United States has taken the blindfold off "Lady Justice" and tipped the scales upside down to interfere with the election of the next President. This is a sign that the current administration and Liberal Democrat Congress have chosen to forget about the laws of our country and the protection of our citizens, and once again, we are back to the rules of the old West.

The only saving grace that stands in the way of this mob mentality is the Supreme Court. To survive, it may be necessary for the Supreme Court to step out of its traditional rules and save America from itself.

Again, these are just my satirical opinions, but change must happen, even if it involves divine intervention.

Chapter Eleven

Dr. Ulyses Stuckum Commentary

Commentary by Dr. Ulyses Stuckum

"Some Folks Need a Bath"

A

t this point I think we need to slap a couple of hornet's nests.

So, it's time to give some attention to Fani Lewis and, the epitome of over-inflated pride... Leticia.

SomeFolks Need a Bath

Back in the old West, water was like gold, and many areas didn't have much gold unless a creek was nearby. Folks didn't have much water, especially hot water, so they had to do their best.

Back then, if you were lucky, you got a hot bath maybe once a month, but everybody in the family had to use the same wash tub and water. The water had to be boiled one pan at a time, usually on a wood fire. Yep, it got pretty friendly by the end.

The house had a pecking order (something we learned from the chickens). This was the usual rule: Dad always got to bathe first, followed by Mom, then the children, and finally the baby.

I imagine it was like putting the baby in a tub of room-temperature chili. When the baby was done, all the kids would drag the tub outside and pour it out on the ground because it wasn't good for much else. That's where the term 'throwing the baby out with the bath water' came from.

When wrestling with pigs, plan to get dirty.

People can get stinky when they wallow in the mud with the pigs. But that's what many lawyers do 24/7/365. Sometimes being covered with all that mud and pig poop tend to change the wallowing lawyers. All that pig poop tends to change the way they think,... or don't.

Still, not all lawyers are bad, even though they are trained to wallow in the mud and pig poop during law school. Some have told me that a law license is really a license to "steal" from folks who don't have one and have no idea what the laws really say. Lawyers always get their fingers in the writing of laws, which means that only lawyers can understand the gibberish brought before our elected representatives vote on becoming laws. That's why pig poop and bad laws smell very similar.

We can't leave this topic without talking about Fani and Letitia

For just a few minutes, let's talk about Fani, a "prosecutor" of national fame who stomped into the courtroom like a petulant Banty Rooster ready to whip a roomful of turkey vultures who were more than ready for some fresh legal road kill to hit the pavement.

Bantam Roosters are rather small. But their delusional minds think they're big, powerful, and could never be eaten by the big, bad wolf or a turkey vulture. **_Delusion_** is a favorite place to hide from the reality of self-believed inferiority. Projecting a persona that 'I'm in control of this place ' emotionally projects to everyone else just how 'out of control' that person is feeling.

During the courtroom showdown, evidence was presented against this Banty Rooster, and it was powerful. This "prosecuting attorney" was left with an egg on her face, claiming that she paid cash for everything she did with her employee/boyfriend, so there was no paper trail." When the dust settled, the Judge gave his answer, and it wasn't very good: 'Fire the boyfriend, and then you can go on with your bloodthirsty rampage against the biggest rooster of all,' a delusion Fani had been living under since before being elected county prosecuting "Banty" attorney.

How could a judge bring himself to make this ruling?

It was easy to see that the judge in that trial was adept at holding his nose and ignoring the age-old rule that the court must make judgments that remain "Above even the appearance of impropriety." Hey Judge, 'Impropriety' was all over her actions and this ruling.

This judge must have been a contortionist in a previous life, for while holding his nose before a slew of TV cameras, holding a fist-full of damning evidence, and realizing that he was up for election, he ignored the evidence and said, "Fire the boyfriend, and you get to keep on going after the big blonde Presidential rooster." We'll see if the judge gets a "Fani endorsement" for re-election in that community. My guess is... he will. It's just my opinion.

While we're on the subject of a conflicted AG Prosecutor,

"How do you handle a problem like Leticia?"

Usually, you handle this problem at the ballot box. But remember, AG prosecutors are lawyers, and as stated previously, some lawyers can slip on a mask of righteousness at a moment's notice, followed by a tsunami of multi-syllabic words they learned while reading a thesaurus in the bathroom. Oh, they get really good at using words and pompous body language designed to engender instantaneous fear, anger, rage, and mob tendencies, even when standing behind a pulpit in a Christian church claiming to be believers in the Ten Commandments. (They're not ten suggestions...they're commandments). Still, as if sitting just to the right of The Creator of this universe, they spew hate like a volcano at the moment of eruption. Words coming from the mouth of a prosecutor must be tested against actions to verify the potential for truth.

So, how do you handle a problem like Leticia?

One of the greatest movies ever made is *The Sound of Music*. Having performed on stage since high school, many of the songs from that iconic movie stick in your head. They're written to do that.

Both the tune sticks, and so do the words. So, with the help of Dr. Keith's AI assistant, Mr. Archibald Dumfuddy, we've made some words to go in this Sound of Music song, **How Do You Handle a problem like Maria**? ...the free-thinking nun who could sing like A bird. These are the new words. You plug them into the music that is now playing in your head. Let's see how this turns out.

How do you solve a problem like Leticia?

When she's in court, we're perplexed,

Politicians feel they are vexed,

'Cause they never know which case she'll choose to slam.

Unpredictable as New York weather,

She'll have you bound and tied together.

She's a crusader, she's a schemer, no, she's a sham.

(Verse 2)

She'll out maneuver any foe,

Make the strongest victims bow low,

She could turn a lobbyist into a shiny pearl.

She is cunning. She's extreme.

She's a conundrum. She's a dream.

She's a headache. She's a marvel. But she's Leticia.

(Verse 3)

She forgets all the other suits,

Focused solely on Trump's pursuits,

But the tables turn, and she'll be left in the dust.

Under the bus with Fani and Wade,

Where the loyalty starts to fade,

She's a pawn in a losing game of political lust.

(Chorus)

How do you solve a problem like Leticia?

Blinded by vengeance, she can't see the snare.

How do you save a soul like Leticia?

A pawn in a game,

Soon forgotten,

Left to despair.

(Closing)

Many a truth she chooses to ignore,

Many a lesson she'll learn no more,

How do you make her see,

The consequences of her spree?

How do you guide a lost soul to land?

(Chorus)

Oh, how do you solve a problem like Leticia?

Lost in the currents of hate's command.

How do you save a heart like Leticia?

A prisoner of rage forever a drift in shifting sands.

There's no way to solve a problem like Leticia.

Pray that God will change her, but truly, she's in His hands.

(END)

Manhattan District Attorney Alvin Bragg (A.B.)

If there were a contest for the '*Poster Child of Legal Stink*' it would

have to include a photo of Alvin Bragg. However, I don't want a

photo of this guy in my book (it draws flies that carry stink.). Here's a man elected to enforce the laws of the state of New York, but 'only if he wants to.'

It's for sure he's got a couple of neurons that have given up on the words "honesty", "integrity", and "following the law." In Alvin's mind, everything seems to include the words...if I want to. If a riot breaks out and a few thousand folks run down the center of New York, throw rocks, bullets, or grenades, and ten thousand crystal clear digital photos are captured on the 9,450 video surveillance cameras everywhere, with a wave of his hand, the looters and rioters are all pronounced free without any jail time...for a lack of sufficient evidence. Close-up camera footage can identify the nose hairs pushing through their cheap masks, but the fact that they are dragging an ATM behind their getaway cars with sparks going in every direction...but A .B. waves his hand, and they are all "innocent – insufficient evidence."

New Yorkers better wake up, or there will be only a handful of stupid people left in Manhattan to pay for massive taxes, unsafe subways, and throngs of homeless demanding that they be moved into the penthouse suite of New York's finest hotels because there is not a law Bragg can't ignore, unless the word Trump is attached in some distant, obscure way.

This man is dangerous to the rule of law in New York. It's for sure when someone says, "No one is above the law," that person thinks they are the exception to that pillar of truth.

If New York doesn't get their act together, those tall buildings and expensive fufu restaurants will not have anyone in them. The rule of law gives people confidence in how they can fit in. With this guy in charge, if you do well financially, you become a target...if Bragg deems it so.

So, all you folks who want a $200 steak sandwich for lunch or a $500 cab ride around the block need to pack your bags, turn out the lights on Broadway, and let the rats have the city. Move to Texas, where there are no state taxes...but leave your New York rules there in New York. The rest of you come to economic freedom in Texas or Florida. Oh, one more thing...Alvin Bragg, Letcia or Fani...stay away. You're not invited to freedom.

Vice President Kamala Harris & 'President Wannabe'

Vice President Kamala Harris ...the Democrat Candidate for President

Before I end my commentary on lawyers and the trouble that some create, how could I poke fun at these other shining examples of the Wrong People...Wrong Jobs and leave out our illustrious Vice President, whose competency pales compared to President Joe Biden's?

Where in the world did candidate Biden find Kamala Harris?

For years, America and the world have watched anxiously to see the real **Kamala Devi Harris** bloom like a rogue dandelion on the freshly manicured White House lawn. Unfortunately, the Vice President has never been able to find her roots and continues to cackle her way through, trying very hard to sound qualified to step into the shoes of Mr. Big at a moment's notice. Regretfully, she is not and may not ever be ready for this job or the one that our forefathers designed for the Vice President of the United States.

(I wonder if Hunter Biden is positioning himself for the Democrat VP position?)

What America painfully has seen is that Kamala has mastered the ability to talk down to everyone she meets like they are a bunch of third graders struggling with the existential meaning of frogs. Her lack of relational development and potential as an entry-level Presidential wannabe has been the presumptive reason that most of the country is praying that President Biden holds on to the last strands of his barely functional mental acuity until the end of his first and only term as President. Then America will applaud President Biden as he takes his lifetime membership for free ice cream at Ben & Jerry's and does away with his only real contact to the White House, his teleprompters and audio earbuds connected to his mental handlers and his eternal connection to former President Obama.

Many Americans, including the Vice President, are clueless about how, from 2011 through 2017, she functioned as the Attorney General of California and a U.S. senator from California for four entire years.

But when you look at the dreadful condition, financial ruin, lawlessness, massive open street drug use, and uncontrolled social condition of the State, it may be that Kamala Harris did leave her mark on California. Remember, the Vice President announced that she "ate the word 'NO' for breakfast." She might need to change her diet to another multi-syllabic word like "IHOP-Pancakes-and-Bacon." (Stay away from the "eggs,"or the tendency to cackle at a moment of quasi-stress may happen more often than it already does.)

Kamala attended law school in San Francisco (Wikipedia) (https://www.politico.com/news/magazine/2020/08/ 11/kamala-harris-vp-background-bio-biden-running -mate-2020-393885) and Politico quoted her as saying in 2018, "I'm dealing with this brutal stuff, dog-eat-dog in school, and then I would come home and we would all stand by the toilet and wave bye to a piece of s___t."

Give me a break Joe, did you have your staff run a mental test on her before making the choice for VP running mate? Does her 2018 quote from Politico sound like someone we should hand the nuclear launch codes capable of global destruction?

It is illusive to most observers just what VP Kamala does each week at the White House. She was assigned to be the "Border Czar" and failed miserably. VP Harris was also put in charge of landing the votes to pass the ***For the People Act***. Many Americans don't even recognize that assignment, and few could even talk about what it was about. So, again, VP Kamala has failed to garner even passing support to be VP Harris.

It seems only appropriate to dedicate an original poem to VP Kamala Harris. (Thank you, Mr. Dumfuddy.)

She's the VP, or so they say,
But her gaffes just won't go away,
Trying hard to seem wise and astute,
But her statements often leave us in dispute.
(Verse 2)

From border issues to space debris,

Seems she's lost in a fog, can't you see?

With every stumble, the critics groan,

Wondering if she's really on her own.

(Verse 3)

From laughing off questions to awkward cackles,

Her political dance, oh, how it baffles.

But in the end, it's all just a game,

For her, it's politics not to be blamed.

How do you soften words often mis-spoken?

How do you make people think, "No, she's not just a token."

The truth is very clear to see,

Bless her heart, that's Our Kamala,

The outgoing VP.

(END)

Is America just an idea to be used for our own needs?

Listen up, Buttercup, because this is a truth many folks have forgotten. America is not just a dream to be used and discarded like trash. Everywhere you look, people are using up America and don't have the character to put anything back into this fine country.

The America we know has been bought and paid for by the blood of Americans. According to ***Statista.com***:

In the American CivilWar (1861-1865) 620,000 lost their lives.

In World War II(1939 to 1945) 405,399 died.

In World War I(1917-1918) 116,516 died.

In the Vietnam War(1965-1973) 58,209 died.

In the Korean War(1950-1953) 36,516 died.

In the AmericanRevolutionary War (1775-1783) died.

The War of 1812(1812-1815) 2,000 died.

In the Mexican-American War (1846-1848), 13,283 died.

In the War on Terror(2001 – present) 7,078 died (so far).

And, in the Spanish-American war of 1898, 2,446 died.

Americans died to buy the America we have today. It was a "blood purchase" for the country we enjoy daily. It tears my heart apart to hear people chanting "Death to America." These chants are made by people who left their country to come to America because they have no freedom there. They have no opportunity there, and they only have slavery to bloodthirsty leaders who would never stand for what America allows in the name of "Freedom of Speech."

Time for a big change

It's time for a change, a really big change. Listen up. **I am just one person with an opinion, and this is it: If you don't love America enough to give your life for it to continue being the envy of freedom lovers across the world...go home**.

1)   If you raise a flag of any another country other than America, then I propose we deliver you back to that land.

2)   I propose we harden the border of these United States of America, and should you choose to break into our country without going through the legal process of becoming an American Citizen or being granted entry for verified asylum purposes, then when our law enforcement teams catch you, you will be sent back. <u>You will never be granted entry to the United States from that point forward.</u>

We Americans respect the blood shed by American fathers and mothers, teens who were drafted into the services, and those who worked to support the defense of our country. When our men were called to defend our land, our women took up jobs in defense plants to make the hardware, planes, tanks, and other vehiclesfor the warriors on the front lines of war. It was hard work, but it was forAmerica.

Below is a photo of one of the plants that made the "Hell Diver" fighter plane. I could find only one man in this photo.

*War time women factory
workers*

One day, a young Army officer arrived to teach electrical wiring to the factory women. That young man was Dr. Keith's father, and that's where his mother and father met. After they were married, before long Baby Dr. Keith came along.

When war broke out, a wonderful father had to leave his wife and young child at home and go off to war again. This is the picture just before his daddy left that day.

As they left him at the train station that day; the little boy cried like never before. It was as though his little heart was pulled out through his chest. Would he ever come home again? Will his daddy live through this war? Will he ever forget that day when his father left for war? Those tears can never be forgotten.

LovedOnes pay the price of freedom, too.

The price for protecting America was not just paid by the warriors but also by their families. That's why you don't break into our country, tear it apart, and destroy the memories of those who paid the price to keep this as our home.

Americans love this country enough to stand by these rules we call "laws." We will not allow anyone who wants to consume it or destroy it at will. Hundreds of thousands have shed their blood for this land. They have bought for us the freedom we now enjoy. They've gone to war, leaving family behind. They have lost limbs, they've lost eyes, and for many, the scars of war stay with them, repeating the battles they've survived at night while others peacefully sleep.

Americans have made great sacrifices in blood, sweat, and tears to keep this country alive. For those who really love this land and plan on it being the hope of the world long into the future, there must be a change—a drastic change. The Wrong Person... the Wrong Job will not be tolerated by Americans dedicated to its survival.

If you want to be on the soil of America, you must pay the price to be here.

Let me put it as simply as I can. Our country right now has too many people who have no intention of defending it, contributing to it, protecting it, and, if necessary, dying for it to keep it alive and well. America is a country where you must put back into it to deserve the right to be protected by America. If you are trying to move your broken down and very unfree country into America, we don't want it.

If you wave the flag of the country you left to come here, then you are not committed to being an American. So, go home. Either you are an American, or you're not. It's kind of like being a little pregnant. Either you are or you're not. Make a choice. Make a commitment...or go somewhere else.

To my fellow Americans...pick the side you're on because you cannot straddle and be on both sides of this issue. Whom do you serve, those who want to destroy America or those who want America to be the home of the free and the brave? Are you the wrong person for the wrong job or the right person to be an American?

I'm Dr. Ulyses Stuckum, and that's my opinion.

Chapter Twelve

"An Exclusive Interview with the Spirit of President Joe Biden"

Chapter 4

"An Exclusive Interview with the Spirit of President Joe Biden"

Sometimes, our humanness causes us to say and act in ways totally opposite to what our "inner being" or "spirit" might prefer as an accurate answer. Because of our momentary "need perceptions," we launch forth with responses or actions we often regret. If only we could speak directly to someone's inner being or spirit and receive a response, we may better understand the reason for their words or illogical responses.

Facing a Horns-of-Dilemma and looking for possible answers

Because this book really focuses on the two major components of the political divide facing our country (Republican vs. Democrat; Conservative vs. Liberal), it might be very helpful to get inside the sitting President of the United States, the leader of the Democratic Party, and get straight answers from the Spirit that drives him. Much of America believes that the President only serves big donors, powerful special interests, and an underworld willing to twist laws that need enforcing so that our American society is stable.

I know it's an unconventional approach, but America finds itself in an unconventional position with a myriad of imminent threats, armed conflicts, a damaged economy with raging inflation, a lack of respect for law enforcement, and the prevailing spirit of Americans that our government has been weaponized against key groups, individual Americans, and not to the protection of all Americans and their allies.

This makes us believe that our constitutional republic and our existence as a free society are in perilous danger. This is serious stuff. The appearance of instability in our leadership invites international aggressors to attack our perceived weakness. We cannot be unstable for the long-term survival of our country.

Let me talk to the Spirit that drives the President

So, as unconventional as it may seem, Americans are at a loss for understanding and need serious answers.

As a health journalist who has interviewed hundreds of individuals about health issues, they have always responded with thoughts and words. As an ordained Chaplain, I have served the spiritual needs of humans for years. With advanced training as a *Diplomate in the American Academy of Experts in Traumatic Stress*, I have focused on the trauma people experience when they are stuck in a traumatic situation and they feel they have no power. Quite possibly, it's time to combine these skills and launch forth into uncharted interview territory.

The Interview's biggest challenge

When interviewing the "spirit" of a person, we don't have the luxury of the spoken word with their response. I can ask questions using words, but the answers are given through perceptions from the spirit. Trust me, a person's Spirit can let its feelings be known as it changes the body's physiology, interrupts the mind's focus, and sometimes awakens the person at night when other distractors have been set aside. The Spirit of a person is not always a silent partner.

People often think they can cause the Spirit that drives them to stay quiet and not respond to bad choices that don't fit with the intentions programmed into the human software driving the mind and body. Eventually, the Spirit has its way. We may battle it, but, from a lifetime of working in this area, it is more powerful than words, so this may be a better interview.

My Radio Interview with Jesus

In one of my previous books, titled "My Radio Interview with Jesus," I related a story that took over my nationally syndicated health radio talk show in ways I could have never expected.

That approach worked, so let's try again, with just a slight change. **Here's the deal. This may be a first, so bear with me as we walk a new path for more understanding.**

<u>Warning</u>: I have reached out for this exclusive interview with President Joe Biden's Spirit. This is not a seance or some Voodoo ritual, and there are no Tarot cards or gypsies within a couple of blocks of this location. The interview takes place while the President sleeps in Washington, D.C. He will probably never know that his Spirit was involved in this interview.

You will see the questions and the emotional interchange that takes place.   You be the judge and weigh the responses. Let's see how this goes.

Ladies and Gentlemen, readers, concerned humans across the world, political tyrants with names sounding like Putin, Xi, or other autocratic users of humans for their own political entertainment:

An Exclusive Interview with the Spirit of President Joe Biden

<u>**Dr. Keith**</u> – Good day to all our readers and viewers. From what I have found, today will be a first. Getting to know the heart and soul of one of the free world's leaders is an awesome task. I'm hoping that I am up to this interview because I think getting to know the soul of someone helps us better understand all the human factors and the motivations that go into making monumental decisions affecting literally hundreds of millions of people worldwide.

Today, we will discuss some topics that hopefully allow us a peek into President Joe Biden's soul. There are no note cards, no teleprompter, and no advisors/confidants speaking into a microphone that projects information through tiny earbuds into the president's ears, but the audience can't hear that. Only two are in this room (I think): myself and the Spirit of President Joe Biden.

Mr. President, thank you for agreeing to this somewhat unique interview. As a spirit, I know you have no voice to speak your responses, but I'm a good listener, and no other distractions are going on. So, if you'll help me to be a good translator of your responses, that will help us both. I promise to share what I <u>feel you are communicating to me and my readers</u> as best I can.

Dr. Keith - Mr. President, have you ever given an interview like this one?

Biden Spirit - No, this is a first. The President is in sleep mode, allowing me to break away from my usual nocturnal duties and responsibilities. The "Big Guy" is sleeping.

Dr. Keith - As you and I know, the "Really Big Guy" never sleeps. That's tough for us 'mere humans' to wrap our heads around. But you know that. What are your usual duties and responsibilities?

Biden Spirit - Figuratively speaking, Joe Biden is the car and thinks he is driving the car. My job is to try to influence where the car goes and what the car does while it's awake. Much of my input comes when Joe is asleep. Let's face it: when Joe is awake, people are pulling on him in all directions: advising him, persuading him, using him, and sometimes lying to him. I'm the part of Joe Biden that whispers suggestions from my perspective. When he's asleep or napping, I do my best work. Joe naps a lot.

Dr. Keith – Wow, sounds like a dance of sorts.

Biden Spirit – It is, of sorts. But I am an advisor; Joe makes the call as to how his dance takes place. That "free will" thing is part of my original programming. I can suggest...I can even nag a bit, but Joe leads the dance. He's had 81 years of dancing, and though his body is aging, he still knows how to dance, so who am I to change the dance? He has to want to change the dance. It's complicated.

<u>Dr. Keith</u> – Does President Biden –

<u>Biden Spiri</u>t – Please, for this interview, just call him "Joe".

<u>Dr. Keith</u> – Ok. Does Joe listen to you when you advise him?

<u>Biden Spirit</u>—Well, sometimes. I am competing with all the others, making demands on his dance. Sometimes, he doesn't listen to anyone...even me. But that's pretty common among humans.

<u>Dr. Keith</u> – I've never heard it put just like that.

<u>Biden Spirit</u> – That's why we're having this interview. To help you and others better understand Joe.

<u>Dr. Keith</u> – Thanks, it's helping.

<u>Biden Spirit</u> - You see, his data input circuits are wearing thin. It happens as the car ages. His balance circuits aren't all in the best shape, so he sometimes trips and falls. But inside Joe, he is trying to be a good President in the time he has left. As his data input circuits age, he must depend more on others to help direct his actions. Sometimes that gets him into trouble. Quite frankly, others use him for their purposes, and Joe takes the heat for it. Sometimes, those purposes aren't the most ethical.

<u>Dr. Keith</u> – When he reached that point, why didn't he retire and pass the title of President to the VP?

<u>Biden Spirit</u> – Being President brings a lot of perks and gets lots of attention. He feels needed. I've talked to him about this. Dr. Keith, do you know what it's like to feel that you are not needed on this earth...that your time has passed? That you have no self-worth? It isn't very clear, and to an 81-year-old man, he will do anything possible to continue feeling needed.

<u>Dr. Keith</u> - If he wins another election, he will be 85 when he is forced to step down as President.

<u>Biden Spirit</u> - Oh, wait a minute, time out. Joe's CPAP mask just came off. He really struggles with that mask, but without it, he rarely visits REM Sleep. Please excuse me, but he needs to put that back on to get back into REM SLEEP mode so we can continue our interview. (communicating with Joe Biden) Come on, Joe. Wake up and put that mask back on. Ok good. His Oxygen saturation is now back to normal. We can continue.

<u>Dr. Keith</u> – We were talking about Joe's age, but can we talk about VP Harris?

<u>Biden Spirit</u> – I don't think Joe is very impressed with the VP. Some of his consultants pushed him to find a female who could be selected as VP. But now, after working with her for four years, I don't think he is impressed with her abilities. Joe gave her the border issue and she made a mess of that. I don't see him being that impressed, but she's there. I really can't say much more than that.

<u>Dr. Keith</u> – Let's discuss Joe's choice regarding the border issues.

<u>Biden Spirit</u> – What's your question?

<u>Dr. Keith</u> – What made President Joe Biden decide to open the border to any and all people from across the world, with no vetting at all?

<u>Biden Spirit</u>—OK, this is a hard question, but I knew I should expect it. Joe is surrounded by many advisors. While I see them and hear them, I can only advise Joe. He formed such close friendships with President Obama during his four years as Vice President that he depends heavily on him for tactical and actionable advice.

<u>Dr. Keith</u> – Are you saying that it was President Obama who decided to open the border that created the flood of people from all over the world...even from countries that are our enemies, drugs, and even terrorists coming into our country?

<u>Biden Spirit</u> – I'm saying that President Obama is a very strong influence on Joe. Remember, I'm here to help you understand how Joe works, not to be a snitch.

<u>Dr. Keith</u> – Understood, but Joe is the president. America elected him to make the decisions to protect our country, people, and all parties. People now have great doubt about Joe. That doubt has changed from not wanting Joe as our president to not trusting that Joe intentionally creates illegal means to stay in office.

<u>Biden Spirit</u> – Look, Joe is my primary objective. I can't speak for former President Obama and his motivations. Joe is my job. But let me remind you that President Obama is not the only major influencer in Joe's life. Regarding his cabinet, each has its own objectives. Each is driven by his or her own consciences, fears, and biases. Each has his or her own past and imperfections. While they are supposed to follow Joe's lead, they often don't, and their bad choices reflect Joe's appearance of competency as president.

<u>Dr. Keith</u> – That's the way the system of government works.

<u>Biden Spirit</u> – Let me use an earthly statement.

<u>Dr. Keith</u> – Certainly.

<u>Biden Spirit</u> – "It's like trying to herd cats." They are all trying to go their own ways, do their own things, and deal with the public reactions... and most Americans expect them to be "perfect" in their jobs. They're not perfect. They are humans.

<u>Dr. Keith</u> – Understood. Americans believe that none of the cabinet Secretaries is competent, and they fear that if Joe is re-elected, he'll keep the same V.P., cabinet, and nothing will change or possibly get worse.

<u>Biden Spirit</u> – Again, forgive my use of a human cliché, "The only thing constant is change." Am I communicating here?

Dr. Keith - You are. And I appreciate your helping me better understand. Can you work more with Joe regarding Secretary Mayorkas and his incessant lying?

Biden Spirit—Mayorkas is on my list. Blinkin is another one. The list is rather long, but I have to let Joe sleep a little. It's one thing for Joe to forget things—that's normal for a guy his age—but it's different for him to lie intentionally. Again, cabinet members are not my job. Joe is my prime objective, but you're correct in feeling that they create a lot of stress on Joe.

Dr. Keith – Do Spirits ever get together and try to solve some of these issues?

Biden Spirit – Doesn't work that way. We don't meet for lunch like the Rotary Club.

Dr. Keith – Let's change directions for a few moments.

Biden Spirit – Certainly.

Dr. Keith – When did you start working with Joe?

Biden Spirit – Let me think about how to say this properly. Birth. Actually, before birth. At conception.

Dr. Keith – You've been the spirit of Joe Biden since before birth?

Biden Spirit – It's pretty neat how this works. When Joe's mom and dad decided to have a baby, at the very moment that Joe started being formed inside his mother, God was there. He always is. He reached inside his own massive Spiritual heart, took a tiny piece of his Spirit, and placed it into baby Joe. That piece of God's Spirit, was me.

Dr. Keith – You're 81 years old?

Biden Spirit – I'm much older than that...you wouldn't understand.

Dr. Keith – Probably not.

Biden Spirit—Most can't get their heads around the concept that The Creator of the Universe and all universes has always been around creating, changing, and loving his creations and that He remains close to them during their entire lifetimes.

Dr. Keith – Wait a minute, Lifetimes?

Biden Spirit—Let me say this, and then let's move on. Before long, Joe will wake up, and I need to be there.

Dr. Keith – Understood.

Biden Spirit – The Spirit of God is placed in babies. Mom and Dad help in the physical area, combining their DNA to make a wonderfully unique baby with a purpose for being alive. All humans are original creations. The Creator makes a totally unique body and loans it to people. The Spirit is like the software that runs the body hardware, but it also runs the emotions. Babies don't run themselves. I am the software...better than AI if I do say so myself. God's software makes AI look like it's stupid and running backwards, but it's still pretty good. It's developing. I am connected directly to the Spirit of God himself. Anywhere, any time I'm always connected. Hard to grasp, isn't it? You really don't need to grasp it. Everything that happens is known and influenced by the Spirit of God...the good, the bad, and the ugly. We love those Western's. I know what you are thinking. No, that phrase came long before Clint Eastwood. To use an earthly phrase again, The Creator's mind...is out of this world.

Dr. Keith – I love it. A spiritual sense of humor?

Biden Spirit – Oh, yeah. Where would man be without the ability to laugh at all the mistakes? Every now and then, a pun helps people think.

Dr. Keith – So, the human body is a home where The Spirit of The Creator lives ...a little piece of Him...but just enough... and moves around.

Biden Spirit – Yep! It's a great plan.

<u>Dr. Keith</u> – Are any babies born without a piece of the Spirit of the Creator?

<u>Biden Spirit</u> – No. All babies, adults, women, and men carry the Spirit with them from conception. Even if they deny His existence, He's still with each and every human.

<u>Dr. Keith</u> – How does Joe deal with the issue of abortion on demand? How can someone make a choice to abort a baby and destroy the human home for God's Spirit? If every baby is born for a specific heavenly reason, how can we change the plans and objectives for that child through abortion?

<u>Biden Spirit</u> – Now you're touching on something very important to The Creator. This is an issue which us "inward Spirits" have been communicating with humans about for a very long time. Let me be crystal clear about this. When a baby dies... God weeps. When a human, made in the image of God himself, dies before its time... God weeps. The God-given ability for a man and a woman participate in the creation of a baby is nothing short of a miracle all by itself. It's not an accident. It's a miracle. But the baby cannot survive without the Spirit of God to uphold it during times of pain, to cheer it in times of triumph, and to love His Creation...even when it makes bad life choices on issues that deeply involve The Creator and His plan for humanity.

<u>Dr. Keith</u> – Well now, there's a quote that I must get right. So, how can Joe support abortion on demand?

<u>Biden Spirit</u> – I am an advisor who can whisper or scream my feelings, but Joe decides the dance he will dance. The perceived pressures on this topic alone come from all directions. The quote "My Body...My Choice" is just wrong. It's not your body. It's loaned to you for a purpose. Men and women are loaned their bodies, and they will give them back at the exact moment God chooses. The power of this abortion decision alone can change election outcomes for all the wrong reasons. But the act of abortion also affects spiritual outcomes. It breaks my heart that humans demand the right to end a baby's life, making those little ones nothing more than 'hostages to politics.' A baby is made in the image of the Creator, and that truth is plainly stated in the Holy Bible. Spirits do the best they can but He knew often they need to read it in order to understand how things fit together in life.

Dr. Keith – Thank you for your frankness and willingness to help people understand President Joe Biden. I need to ask you some things about Joe as a father.

Biden Spirit – Parenting is one of the hardest jobs in the world. Most people parent the way they were parented: right or wrong, good or bad. This is why it's so hard to change, even when you see that some parenting styles aren't working and there's a need to change, but the habits are so ingrained that change rarely happens. There needs to be extensive training to have a child. But, then again, that might get parents started, but the real learning begins when you throw in hormones, sex, and the internet. Any of those three things can turn a perfectly normal child into a raving maniac...at times.

Dr. Keith – That's a great observation and so true.

Biden Spirit – I've watched it for 81 years. Joe is a true mixture of his mom and dad, physically and emotionally. Catherine Eugenia Finnegan, Joe's mom, and Joseph Robinette Biden Sr. were married in 1941. His mom preached the importance of family, loyalty, and faith, but her Irish blood turned her into an outspoken hater of the British. Joe loved both his sons and daughter. He lost his first wife and daughter in 1972 to a severe accident when his wife took the children to buy a Christmas Tree. His two sons survived but had serious injuries. When Beau died of cancer, this was yet another serious emotional blow to Joe. Hunter had severe skull damage.

It is probably fair to consider Joe an "enabling" parent. That "enabling" gene stays with you, and sometimes it surfaces when you become president and have the ability to print money or use it to create perceived power.

Dr. Keith - I think the public has noticed that those tendencies may have resulted in some family members taking advantage of Joe by selling access to meeting him and using his political position for significant personal and political financial gain.

Biden Spirit—My job is to advise Joe. Just like in all families, there are very complex relationships that interact with him. To put it mildly, family dynamics affect how individuals perceive themselves inwardly. That affects how Joe acts and reacts to life situations. Enough said on that subject. Joe has always loved animals, and not long ago, he took in a rescue dog named "Major." Taking in a rescued dog is an act of love. They are a life form whose main purpose is to give and receive love. So many of them are mistreated and abused. The Creator is all about "love." "Major" was intended to be loved.

Dr. Keith – Oh yes, that was the dog who made a chew-tory out of many Secret Service Agents guarding Joe.

Biden Spirit – Yeah, that didn't work out well at all. That's why Joe gave up on dogs and adopted a tabby cat named "Willow." I think the Secret Service agents really appreciated when "Willow" came to the White House.

Dr. Keith – Please let me circle back to Joe's decision to open the southern US Border.

Biden Spirit – That was a quick transition.

Dr. Keith – Sorry, was there something else you wanted me to know?

<u>Biden Spirit</u> – No, but we only have a limited interview time.

<u>Dr. Keith</u> - So much damage to America has happened because of that border position created by Joe. Tens of thousands of unaccompanied children have been showing up at the U.S.–Mexico border each year, many being swept into child sex trafficking circles with ties to cartels. Fentanyl trafficking has taken so many American lives, and right now, in America, there is enough illegal fentanyl to kill every man, woman, and child many times over. How can he deal with this? Has he ever considered going before the American public and just saying, "Sorry, this was a bad idea?"

<u>Biden Spirit</u> – Joe has never been very good about admitting fault for decisions that ended up being rather tragic, even after unquestionable evidence in the media has proven them wrong. It's just not in his set of abilities. But we've talked about this. I mean, I've talked and prayed that Joe listened.

<u>Dr. Keith</u> – Rather stubborn?

<u>Biden Spirit</u> – Rather. I'd better stop there. Listen... Joe is stirring, and I need to get back to him. I hope this has been helpful.

<u>Dr. Keith</u> – It has. However, I know there will be lots of feedback when I present this to my readers. There will be some positives, but there will possibly be a whole truckload of negatives. But that's ok. We tried something new, and I think it worked. Let me leave you with one final thought before you whisk yourself back to Washington, D.C., and resume your duties. If you should have any follow-up thoughts or other topics you'd like to help me and a few billion humans on this earth to understand better, can you reach out...in a spiritual kind of way...and can we talk like we did today?

<u>Biden Spirit</u> – Let me check with my boss on that.

<u>Dr. Keith</u> – Joe?

<u>Biden Spirit</u> – No, that would need to be decided by a much higher power. We'll see because I know being better understood is high on the importance scale. I know how to reach you.

<u>Dr. Keith</u> - I want you to have the final word, a piece of wisdom, please.

<u>Biden Spirit</u> - Don't expect "perfection" from anyone because humans are not "perfect"—not President Biden, not Donald Trump... nobody on earth. Each person alive makes decisions based upon their perceptions of survival at the time. Those perceptions change often. Think about that, and the ups and downs of life just might be easier to understand. Oh, and listen to the Spirit inside you. It's there for a reason. No one likes to be alone in life. Now you know...they never are. Trust me, this is not an easy job.

<u>Dr. Keith</u> – "Thanks."

Chapter Thirteen

"An Exclusive Interview with the Spirit of President Joe Biden" (SPLIT)

Chapter Fourteen

"An Exclusive Interview with the Spirit of President Joe Biden" (SPLIT) (SPLIT)

"Commentary by Dr. Ulyses Stuckum"

"Time to wake up, Buttercup. We are in the middle of a political war."

"Wake Up"

It surprises me how many Americans can sleep their way through a war. With all the violence, hate speeches, universities 'of higher education' falling apart at the seams, congress spending money like it never has to be paid back; political payoff's to buy votes, hate for our police, and inviting thugs, rapists, jihadists, and folks openly dedicated to the destruction of our lives, our country, and our way of life...wake up. We are in the middle of a political war, and there are victims of this war lying all around us.

If you've ever looked closely at the main promotional photo I use, you'll see that I always have a brain in one hand. That's my prop to get folks to wake up and realize that there is absolutely no difference between not having a brain and having one but not using it. The result is the same.

Didn't know it was missing

During my anatomy class, I could slip out a human brain to use as my prop. The brain in the photo is one from a 50-year-old lawyer who taught university students that they didn't have to do anything after graduation but move back in with their parents, reconnect the umbilical cord to mom, and try to crawl back into mom's womb and do nothing.

Well, guess what? There is no 'womb with a view.' The umbilical quick disconnect has been removed, and if you don't work and make this planet just a little better than it was the day before you arrived, you don't get to eat.

The professor/lawyer obviously wasn't using his brain for anything productive, so I slipped it out when he was not looking. The problem is this: he has not even noticed that his brain is missing and floating in a vat of water I carry when speaking at conventions, professional meetings, and high schools. (I love to speak at high schools. It's nothing but a 'cauldron of hormones' and conflicting attitudes on subjects that will not allow students to live one extra day on this earth.) Remember, in high school, each student's head is filled with what I call "Brain-Jell-o®." Don't depend on AI to do your thinking. It has a mind of its own.

If you look at the brain of a 14-, 15-, or 16-year-old on a microscopic level, the brain parts are all there, but they're just not connected completely. It looks a lot like Jell-o (no disrespect intended for the makers of Jell-o.) Oh, they can process some information, but they don't understand the more you use your brain... the better it works.

Now it seems like schools teach it's better "to feel things" than "to seek wisdom" and act on that.

Forgive my comments. In my opinion, the White House looks like it's being run by a large bunch of geriatric teenagers. They don't seem to look ahead on anything involved in running our country, and many wear shirts with "D's" on them. The "D's" stands for Democrat, dimwit, or dipstick. You decide. But forget words and promises you may hear. Promises are words with no action. Based your belief more on their actions, not their words. One of my best friends, a special forces veteran who rescued Congressional hostages captured when they visited foreign countries and just had to go to dangerous places. He called them "wingnuts." It's not a bad term.

A large percentage of the country believes that many of the finest democrats in leadership positions right now have never gone beyond high school in brain development, and they usually function like a gang of dimwit wingnuts. You define it.

It is time to focus on the upcoming election or face some pretty bleak issues

If you have not yet looked, there's a really important election just around the corner. It may be the most pivotal election of a lifetime. In the past, elections were usually similar to playing football. One team runs the ball for a series of downs, and then the other team gets the ball. Those days are over. Now, Democrats play to win, even if it means playing dirty to win "future power.

Republicans believe elections are about "leadership." "Democrats" believe elections are about Power.

If you think that all the pieces of the election are 'on the table right now,' you're stupid. You're delusional. Wake up! There are pieces of your life being auctioned off to the highest bidders, and you don't even know you are on the market for sale.

Here's a dose of reality. What if Joe Biden decides that this election is too hard to fight? What if he resigns or becomes mentally incompetent to the point that Democrats consider him a major liability? Well, I got that one right. Now the only one who has proven she can be used and will sing the Liberal Democrat song is Kamala Harris. She destroyed California as Attorney General. She did the worst job ever in running for President previously and dropped out in disgrace. So who did the elite power brokers of the Liberal Democrat party select after Joe Bidon was given his place under the bus...Kamala.

Democrats opened their box of "Tokens" and select some poor-victim to be chewed up by the last minute game change. Let's look into that box of "Tokens" for the possibilities that might show up for the political carnage that awaits. In that box of "Tokens" were these folks and none of them have any leadership qualities but aren't ripe for manipulation by Liberal Democrat Party power mongers.

Governor Gavin Newsome – Now there's a token Democrat who looks good, slick as a discount life insurance salesman at a geriatric convention, and has already screwed up the state of California so badly that if you elect him, overnight America will look exactly like the mess of California. He's already been to the White House and measured the Oval Office for drapes. Wrong person ...wrong job...wrong ethics... and wrong for America. Let him run Haiti and see how he does there. (Sorry Haiti!)

Deplorable Hillary Clinton - Oh Lord, will this person ever go far enough away with her billions of dollars and realize that once you illegally smash your government cell phones and acid wash the hard drives of your computer to hide everything you have done, America fully understands, under the bus is where you will be seated. Wrong person...wrong job...wrong ethics...and wrong for America. Under the bus with Newsome.

Michelle Obama—now, why would this pretty lady give up the peace and serenity of living with Barrack in the lap of luxury and trade that in for 24/7 filled with stress off the charts? She would be reminded of everything that she ever did that was even the slightest wrong in her life, and Barrack would always be in the background, trying to pull the puppet strings to control her in the Oval Office, like he did with President Joe Biden would do with Kamala.

She would never get a moment of peace. By the way, sleeping with Barrack does not give you the skillset to be President. This is not about the color of her skin. It's about how the Democrat party will control her until she's had enough, and then 'under the bus' she'll go

with Hillary, Newsome, and Biden. One thing we know for sure is that the Democrat Party 'will eat its own people as soon as it can't use them anymore to gain and control power.' Michelle, keep your life of luxury. You've survived raising teenagers and living with Barrack; don't take the bait the Liberal Democrat power brokers might offer. Wrong person...wrong job...wrong for America...and wrong for Michelle.

Preparing the Republican/Conservative Brain for the conflict of an election

Dr.Keith and I think an awful lot alike on so many issues. We say things differently. He's a city boy; I can't hold that against him. On this topic, we sing the same song, and it needs to be sung in chorus by all who want America to survive.

He once told me that one of the joys of being a political satirist is that he uses a wide variety of tools, words, and concepts to awaken an emotion that causes readers and listeners to move on important issues. This is one of those times. What I am about to describe is reality. It's been hidden right before our collective eyes.

Republicans and independents are tired of high inflation, high cost of gas, and of having liberal Democrac edicts pushed down our throats like a goose being used to make 'Patefoie grass.'

Republicans are tired of watching the country fall apart, but we have to realize that we are playing by a different set of rules than the other side. With Liberal Democrats, they gain power by not telling the other side what the rules are until they have become fixed in laws. Remember the words of Nancy Pelosi when she said before a major vote in the House of Representatives. **"I guess you'll have to vote on the bill...in order to see what's in the bill."** Then she laughed as though it was a joke. It was no joke. She was playing by a totally different set of "rules" that have always been in place...in the minds of Republicans/Conservatives.

<u>Republican mindset</u>: The rules of society are embodied and protected by the laws we vote upon, with both parties having a say, passing, and the President signing to become the law of the land.

<u>Democrat mindset:</u> The rules/laws of society can be changed, altered, ignored, interpreted according to what we want them to be...justified totally by our quest for power. Once obtained, we structure the law of the land, and everyone else becomes our subjects.

Why do we keep trying to change Liberal Democrats into becoming Republicans? It's different DNA. Chickens have wings, but that doesn't mean they can fly.

Rodeos: viewed by Republican Eyes

Example: For decades, in Rodeos, we've learned that when it comes to bull riding, the cowboy plops down on the back of the bull with his face toward the head of the bull. The hand of the cowboy is tied to the bull to help him stay on when the action starts.

A flank strap is put around the back of the bull. A "helper" jerks the strap hard when the cowboy says ready. That tickles the side of the bull. Using the flank strap is much easier than having the cowboy reach back during the somewhat challenging effort to stay on the top of the bull and tickle his sides. Tickling the sides, Mr. Bull makes him laugh, but as he laughs, he does anything he can to buck, throw his legs back, and try to make the tickling stop. For those of you who think that the bulls are being abused or that the flank strap is driving the testicles of the bull up into places they were not designed to be...you're wrong. The "flank strap" is just a "tickle strap," but it does put the bull into "action mode," bucking whoever is "tickling him" and poking him in the sides with the spurs to persuade "the tickler" to get the heck off his back.

Oh, and by the way, the bull believes whoever is tied to his back must be causing that tickle and quickly needs to be shown what a couple of well-placed horns of a 2,000-pound bull looking for that terrible tickling... can do.

For comparison, let's call the "Republican/Conservative mindset" of this friendly interaction between cowboy and bull in a game called "Rodeo." No harm was done to the bull, even though the cowboys tend to walk a little funny after flying high in the air and landing on their butt. Why can't more of America be cowboys?

A Democrat View of Rodeos

Now, just for the sake of persuasion, let's look at this age-old game of Rodeo through the eyes of a Liberal Democrat/Left-Wing/congressperson/wingnut.

Everyone in the stands thinks this is a game with Mr. Wooly Bully. And because I know I am an entitled Congressional Democrat/Left-WingCongressperson/wingnut, I can change the rules of the game anytime... when I want. I don't have to tell anyone else until the game is over. Here are some rules Liberal Democrats might change... by Executive Action to make things really interesting and fair.

1) The cowboy must ride the bull facing toward the butt end of the animal.

2) The cowboy's hand is tied to the flank strap and really tickles the bull even more. Because of the severe tickling, the bull bucks harder. The backbones of the bull now put the cowboy's testicles in a crunch match as he's thrown around at the whim of the bull.

3) The flank strap can only be made from a super soft, Russian-imported yak pelt, which tickles the bull even more and makes him smile. Unemployed FBI Agents check the bull to make sure that the Rodeo is complying with animal protection laws. Bulls have rights, too.

4) Before each ride, the horns on the bull must be professionally sharpened to give the bull a life-and-death advantage over the testosterone-filled cowboy who has never faced a tickled bull in a 'menopause moment. (You say there are no female bulls? You're wrong, transitioning bulls are very sweet animals.)

5) The cowboy has to wear a blindfold and is not told about the rules that have been changed... until the gate opens. I guess the cowboy had "to vote for the bill (bull)... in order to find out what's in it."

This is what I call the "Pelosi strategy" in action (and she was the third step down from being the President of the United States). If that doesn't scare you, you are ready to walk down the streets of New York and see how long you survive.

During the Election cycle, Conservatives have got to 'sharpen their horns and brains with a new set of mental adjustments. It's time to form the right attitude for elections.

1)   Electing a president or congressperson is a very serious action. If you don't think it is serious, you end up with AOC or the Biden/Harris fiasco, which means four years of executive orders designed to go around the laws that have been on the books for hundreds of years based on 'the people's will.' Inflation, social instability, forced transition to electronic vehicles that self-ignite and can't be extinguished by fire crews (if there are any left), and universities that are void of intelligence. Our laws have instructed the government how they are to act and set needed boundaries on the 'out-liars' who would try to take over the American citizens.

2) During an election year, we must realize that Democrats have set aside the term "American," designed to unify us into one country of citizens. During the election year (and some would claim it to be year-round), they are Democrats/left-wing wingnut combatants capable of the most unthinkable, un-American, illegal, immoral, dastardly, and sub-human acts against Americans...to win power. This is all about power acquisition and conquest. (Who in their right mind would otherwise open the borders of safety for America and invite in a few million "migrants" who bring drugs, weapons, gangs, cartels, and children who become "lost" into child sex slavery and exploitation, and bringing in dump trucks of drugs that kill American young people every day? What moral leader would destroy our economy, bribe our citizens, drive up inflation, and effectively kill our own use of fossil fuels that can make our country independent but instead make us dependent on our enemies?) What true American would do those

things? In the quest for ultimate power and control...an enemy combatant has done that.

3) Never underestimate the opponent and their willingness to act outside the law for survival to rule another day.

4) **Stop calling Democrats "Progressives." They are not pro-gressive. They are re-gressive.** They move us away from freedom and into a wide variety of slaveries.

Liberal Democrats are not Pro-gressive...stop calling them what they are not!

5) This year, over 100,000 Republican/Conservative election observers armed with cameras holding empty storage chips, recording devices, and inquisitive eyes will be present to watch and capture evidence of even the slightest voting impropriety. They will put a little duct tape over the computer reset port on the back of the voting computer so things can't be changed with the tip of a pencil.

6) This year, cemeteries will be closed to voting...and live Americans must only be voting. No dead folks voting...let them rest. That ain't racist, so stop using that term. But watch out for an executive order that instantly makes migrants American citizens by edict. (Even Democrats realize that it takes time for the Supreme Court to act in protection of American rights. So don't be surprised.)

7) Presidents use laws to protect citizens and safeguard our country. They don't create the laws. A tyrant's presidency can damage America in ways that will take decades to repair.

8) Don't be surprised if the "presidential privilege of clemency" is used dastardly to protect the guilty rather than to save those improperly condemned in the courts.

Americans must dig deeper before they believe what people say: people "show" what they believe with their actions.

Americans listen up...If it's a pig, call it a pig, no matter how much lipstick you put on that pig, or if someone renames the pig and calls it a"dove."...it's a pig. If people get offended by the truth, they deserve AOC. Remember, she has just made a big jump from being a bartender to being a member of Congress, and it looks like she's going to make mistakes. She has never said, "You know, folks, I was wrong, and I should have never pushed a green new deal "poop" on everyone. It'll never work." If you ever hear her say that, cover your wallet and hide your children. She's acting...it's her next job!

If we become unable or unwilling to call a pig...a pig...then we deserve to say goodbye to America.

Time to toughen up for this election

This will be a tough election, so buckle up, buttercup (I love that phrase). You must change how you think about those "temporary political combatants." Once the election is over, allow a new America to be born and sweep away a lot of the garbage. Birthing a new baby has never been easy and there is usually just a touch of ....discomfort.

This is the question we need to be pondering: how fast can we get millions of folks from other countries who hate this country, wearing their foreign flags, chanting death to America, fully equipped with cell phone cameras to gather evidence against our border patrol agents while getting jobs as professors, students, or 'professional disruptors' in our "used to be" best universities...to go back home where they really belong...and start healing our country?

These are my opinions—and the opinions of hundreds of millions of Americans who want to keep the real America around for our families, children, and grandchildren long into the future.

Dr. Ulyses Stuckum

Chapter Fifteen

Curse Your Children

Chapter 5

"Curse Your Children!"

When I read the Bible, it seems pretty clear that our Creator does not want bad things to happen to children. In fact, He goes so far as to drive that point home by saying, 'If you cause one of these little ones to go astray, you get a really heavy millstone hung around your neck, and you get dropped into the deepest part of the sea.' It doesn't take a lot of intelligence to see that He means business when it comes to kids—eternal business.

Big people make big mistakes

As a young doctor fresh out of school, I can still remember one of the biggest mistakes I ever made in practice. Like most of my mistakes in life, they have burned their essence into the deepest parts of my brain. They humble me every time I think I can walk on water.

The patient was a forty-year-old, attractive woman who had come to me for help. My unexpected lesson was delivered during the initial get-acquainted visit, just before I reviewed her health history.

When fresh out of professional school, doctors often have a subliminal delusion that they can handle anything. The discussion went something like this:

Dr. Keith – Thanks for coming to our practice and giving us a chance to help you. Please tell me a little about you. Are you married?

Patient – Oh yes. I have a wonderful husband named George.

Dr. Keith – Do you work...or are you a housewife?

That's when I saw an instantaneous change in her expression. Her pupils dilated like you would expect in a 700-pound Black Bear whose cubs were about to be attacked by a hungry coyote. Her face turned red, and the innocent, socially stupid young doctor got his first lesson in choosing the right words during a patient interview.

Patient – Don't you think that a housewife works? Don't you think being a mother is a "real job?"

My assistant covered her face because she knew what had happened would leave a mark on me that would last a lifetime. It did. I didn't even feel the knife pass through my neck as my head figuratively fell from my shoulders and rolled innocently across the floor.

While I was mentally focusing on getting to her health history, I had voluntarily walked into a massive area of quicksand, and I was going under. After about 15 minutes of eating multiple plates of crow (no, it doesn't taste like chicken), she finally dismounted my dismembered carcass, and I apologized profusely for my immature choice of words. I've never forgotten that moment and the reality of my confused assumptions.

The Best Birth Control Technique Ever

By far, being a parent and raising children who can survive in this world is the most complicated job of all. On ***America's Dirtiest Jobs*** TV show, I don't think they've ever produced a show on the realities of being a parent. It's more than holding down lunch as you pour out the contents of a newborn diaper. If Mike Rowe ever did that one, without a doubt, that show would be "the best birth control technique ever created."

The "Brutal Truth" Birth

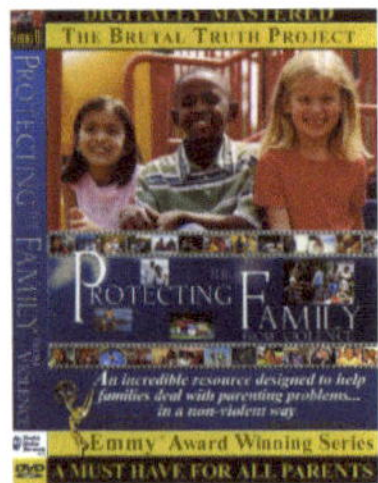

In 2005, my co-producer, Carrie Woliver, and I, along with an incredible multi-emmy award-winning indie TV filmmaker named Rick

Christie, created a TV documentary series titled ***The Brutal Truth Project***. The TV series started with ***The Brutal Truth: A Violence Documentary***, which won three ***Emmys*** from the ***National Academy of TV Arts and Sciences***. The second show in the series was titled ***The Brutal Truth: Protecting the Family from Violence.*** I hosted this TV show and was the screenwriter for both shows. As we began our field research for each show, it became obvious to me that there are no easy answers to the question of the use of violence.

In preparation for these shows, our research looked at violence and its effects on the family from 2001 through 2006. At that time, our team went to the poorer areas of Houston for some answers.

What is Violence?

I recall interviewing a group of 13-17-year-old black young men and asking them the question: "What is violence?" One of the young men said he didn't feel that it was violence when his father or mother beat him with their fists. While another felt that having a friend shot and killed by someone was violent. And a large number of the young men said that they had experienced a close friend who was a murder victim of a violent attack.

When I compare the violence occurring at that time to the violence that impacts the family today in 2024, there is absolutely no comparison. The jobs of a mother and father today are off-the-chart and exponentially more difficult.

This reality raises the key question: **How do we protect our children from the belief that they can use violence as the default response to aggression by someone else?** I've experienced it for myself.

I recently drove to the grocery store on one of many 'honey-do' projects. While I wasn't going slowly, I was not breaking the speed limit either. Out of nowhere, a small car raced toward the rear of my vehicle and leaned on the horn for about two hours (exaggerating just a bit). Then he revved his engine, passed me on the driver's side, and attempted to push my car off the road. I pulled over to prevent an accident. With his car now in front of me, the young man opened the back door to his vehicle and retrieved a baseball bat, then headed straight for the front of my car.

Well, I was born, but not yesterday. I could tell that my 2017 Ford F-150 was about to incur some major damage, and it might include my windshield or me.

In Texas, it's probably safe to just assume that every woman has a 45-caliber pistol in her purse and every man has something like my ***Springfield Armory, Hellcat 9 mm, with a green laser sight***. I'm very proud of my Hellcat 9mm. (Remember my history of being a police chaplain. On the range, I was very proud of how I could beat many of the officers in target practice.)

Faced with the eventuality of my truck becoming a huge paperweight, I raised my Hellcat 9 mm, set the butt of the gun on my steering wheel, and pointed to it, screaming, "You want to go shooting with me?

The attitude on the young man's face went from flaming hot to ice-cold in a matter of milliseconds. The blood drained out of his head, and I prayed I wouldn't have to deliver him to the doorstep of The Creator for his private conference on "bad choices while on earth."

He quickly put his bat back into the car and drove off. I continued to pray for him...and me, for another 4-5 minutes. I kept asking myself, should I have shown him my Bible with the red letters highlighted, or did I do the right thing showing him how proud I was of my Hellcat 9mm...and offering to take him to the firing range? If physical violence is the initial response to aggression by someone else, that perception may be just one serious "curse" carried by our children as they grow up, get married, and have children of their own.

Kids are tuned into lots of media

Violence comes in a variety of packages, some openly recognizable while others are just under the surface but instill a violent response. Also, the fear of violence gives the aggressor the emotional control they may be seeking.

Recently (2024), I spoke to a young man who was ending his Junior High school experience and was assigned to a school where there had been a recent shooting at the hands of another young student. The student who was shot died of his injuries. In that school, there was no on-site police presence, and daily fights occurred between students and gangs.

How can we knowingly place students in an atmosphere where violence happens more often than does education? It's commonly known among students that often the worst discipline the shooter gets is "juvie," and their records are expunged because of being a minor. What is the deterrent? Did I mention that there are no easy answers?

The Media often makes the problem of Violence worse for children

Being in the media as a nationally syndicated health radio talk show host afforded me the chance to see how the media can do good...but often just makes the problem of violence worse. I suppose it is fair for me to raise the point that the news is filled with violence. Newsrooms have a mantra, "If it bleeds...it leads."

Movies with violent scenes always draw the attention of viewers. Young people have great difficulty remembering that scenes in violent movies are "just stories with blood that looks real but isn't." In some of the younger viewers, the scenes appear so real that their minds consider them "real." The bodies respond as though they are "real" even when they know it isn't real.

In my opinion, this is the most challenging reality: young people rarely listen to the words parents use, but they watch what the parents <u>do</u>...and most often, that's what the young person considers OK. They become numb to the reality of death, almost as though the shooting was a game, and the only loss was points on the scorecard. Then, when the game begins again, the opponent miraculously comes alive again for another round. If a young person sees violence in the home, it's painful deep inside the child, but it sends a message that this is the appropriate way to act. That plants a dangerous seed that can grow into a condition known as transgenerational violence.

The Biggest Pressure is on the parents.

That puts massive pressure on parents to groom themselves in respect, openly discuss topics of disagreement, and "time out" when emotions get too high. In a single-parent household, it is a monumental task to maintain a peaceful, safe environment where young people can go through the developmental stages that lead to adulthood. But if you don't...**you curse your children**.

Bad Assumption: If you're smart, you don't get mad.

On the news, we have been overwhelmed by violent demonstrations involving quasi-elite, highly educated college students shouting for the genocide of whole populations motivated by explosive hate under the guise of protests.

"Smart" has nothing to do with the violent reactions. Violence is an emotional response. It's not logical. In the battle between emotions and logic...emotions almost always win.

A college student with straight A's at an Ivy League university, holding a ball bat and full of emotion, finds it really hard to stop himself/herself in mid-swing of the bat and say...you know if I break this $3000 window, the cameras that are recording me are going to be able to identify me because of the AI facial recognition software. I will get captured, thrown in jail, and have to pay money to get out of jail. Based on this assessment...I think I'll just put this bat down and go home...and miss the pepper spray.

It doesn't happen like that. Violence and rage take over and that erases logic.

You are either "learning" or "teaching."

My dad told me, "At any moment you are alive, you are either learning...or you're teaching." Either you experience the pepper spray in your eyes or the broken jaw from a police baton, or another student is watching you make bad choices, and they are making your bad choice, theirs. I don't know if Dad wrote that or if it was handed down to him, but it's true.

Violence is all around...so how do we change the trajectory of hate that seems to be taking hold? Like it or not, we are cursing the children who watch it on TV, in the social media or in online communication with other kids. How do we change the habitual response of violence?

Chapter Sixteen

Curse Your Children (SPLIT)

Little League Baseball Player Hit in the Head by a fast-ball

It was a high-pressure, **little-league** baseball game between Texas and Oklahoma. At bat was a young man from Oklahoma whose life was about to change forever. The Texas pitcher wound up and let a fastball stream toward the plate, but although it was fast, it was not accurate. Before the Oklahoma batter could move, the fastball struck the side of his head, but the Helmut took much of the impact. The Oklahoma player helplessly fell to the ground, holding his head in both hands and tears streaming in all directions. On the mound, the young Texas pitcher was also in tears, openly sobbing for the pain he caused by the poorly directed ball.

Slowly, the Oklahoma batter moved to first base, holding his helmet. That's when he looked up and noticed the Texas player's deep remorse for the pain he had caused.

That's when "the miracle" happened. The young man on first base slowly walked to the pitching mound to even the score with the Texas pitcher, but when he arrived, rather than throwing punches, the young Okie put his arms around the pitcher to ease the pain he was feeling.

My eyes filled with unconscious tears at that miracle. The young Okie found a secret lesson within him and cared more about the Texas boy than he did about himself. Wow! Everyone who watched it learned the lesson to the depths of their hearts. He taught us through his actions.

Much of the time, violence is a choice. These two little leaguers taught people across the world about their choices. It's a choice made in a split-second but reverberated with goodness that will live on for decades. If you want to see the video, go to: ((https://www.youtube.com/watch?v=INQa4LSzcuY). See if you are moved with this lesson.

One final note: If you are attacked, you must respond, not just to defend but to create the first injury in the attacker that will stop the attack. "Defense only" just might get you seriously injured or possibly dead. Defense is just the beginning response, but it must quickly transition to an offensive move to stop the attack. Unfortunately, these days, this message must be passed on to our young people through combat training.

Often, the knowledge that we have the potential and training to stop an attack changes the chemistry within the responder. Unfortunately, our world has transitioned into a very violent place to live.

The Restaurant Scene: A great burger

Let me share one more personal experience where a potential violent exchange was turned away with words and turned into a learning experience for the verbal attacker.

In Texas, there are many restaurants where one can enjoy a great hamburger; we can't hide that from our cardiologist. I had just arrived at one of my favorite restaurants for one of those remarkable burgers.

Standing in line to place my order, I noticed an attractive black woman. She was very well-dressed and wearing a large and colorful hat. She was smiling and appeared to be waiting for a friend to join her for lunch.

As I entered the serpentine line for my time to order, I came close to where she was standing. I did the "Texas gentlemanly thing" and offered for her to get in line before me. She declined.

I stepped up to the counter and ordered my burger. That's when I noticed the woman standing next to me. After I ordered, she told the person taking the order, "...and I'll have the ribeye medium rare, a baked potato, and a side salad with blue cheese dressing." The order taker took down her order below my burger order.

I told the order taker, "Oh, excuse me, we are not together." That's when the woman began her unexpected attack on me.

"Do you mean that you will not buy me food?"

Being from Texas, I tried the gentlemanly response. "Mam, we are not together, so our orders should be separated."

Her response left no question in my mind; she was there to create a scene and stir up trouble in front of all the people still in line. As if in suspended animation, the waitstaff was aghast and nervously waiting for her next incendiary launch. I knew it was coming, so I turned and looked her in the eyes. That's when she said, "I guess you are a racist."

The gauntlet was set, the trap had been sprung, and my foot was the target. I turned to the woman, smiled, and said, "Oh, no, mam, I am a police chaplain, and some of my best friends are black, and I work with them daily. But I am no racist."

Since her first attack didn't work, I prepared mentally for her next attack.

"Well, I am hungry, and you won't buy me food? Besides, I am a minister, too, and I don't have any money." She was adept at using massive loads of guilt to get what she could from people, and tried to ensure it landed on my plate.

Again, smiling, I responded as the entire room of 20 or so onlookers watched the stand-off at the counter. "Mam, then we work for the same God. I know you'll work something out...but let's get this straight. <u>I am not going to buy you food today</u>, and that's it."

"Why?"

"If you had just said, "Look, I am hungry. I don't have any money. Would you buy me some food?" I would have said, "Sure. Maybe not the ribeye, but you would get food. But, mam, you then crossed the line and played "The Racist Card" and tried to intimidate me into buying you food...and with that, you cemented your fate. If I had given in and bought you food to try to prove that I am not a Racist, then you would have been positively rewarded for doing a bad job of laying guilt on me. If that had worked, you would think, 'Hey, I can use this again on my next victim.' So, you sealed your own fate with the word "racist." Ma'am, I am the executive editor-at-large and vice president of an all-black news magazine. You picked the wrong target. Now you have a wonderful day and don't use that "racist" card...because with me, you will lose every time."

That was a learning experience for her, all the people who were watching, and for the lady taking the orders for food. The lady walked away from the counter and back into the restaurant, looking for her next target. The sweet young lady at the counter handed me the ticket for my burger and said, "I'm so sorry, sir." I told her, "You can't control what people say or do. We need to pray for her, but it was up to me to respond to her attack."

The next time I entered the restaurant, the same young lady who worked the ordering desk recognized me and said, "We had a staff meeting about what happened to you. You did good. Now, what do you want on your burger?"

People are always watching, listening, and learning. I don't want to curse anybody, including children. I believe we learn best through experiential learning. That day, a whole bunch of people were in class at that restaurant. By the way, it was a great burger!

I had better stop there and let Dr. Stuckum share his thoughts.

Chapter Seventeen

Dr. Ulyses Stuckum Commentary

Dr. Ulyses Stuckum Commentary

"Curse your Children" A West Texas Wiseacre

A long time ago, when I was a little boy, it may surprise you that I was a little bit of a wiseacre. OK, a significant wiseacre.

I went to a school and a small Texas town where the teachers didn't take any crap from kids. We knew we couldn't get away with it, but being kids, we figured we'd try anyway.

There was a shop teacher, a Navajo Indian descendant, who effectively let us know when we stepped over the boundaries. It was called a "hand-warmer," and when the teacher said, "You've gone too far. Come over here and give me your hand. Not minding the shop teacher was not an option.

And we knew we were about to have an "S.L.E." (Significant Life Experience). That means you will remember it for most of your life. We did.

He would take the hand of your choice, palm up, and bend the fingers back just a little bit, just enough to expose the fleshy palm. He would reach in his top desk drawer. That's where he kept the "Hand-Warmer paddle. It was a small paddle just about the size of the hand, and he would say, "Do you know what you did that was wrong?"

We would dutifully respond, "Yes, sir."

Then he would say, "This is gonna hurt you more than it does me, but I want you to think about it. This will help you remember that you went too far."

He would lay down the hand-warmer paddle, and the entire class would have to watch as each student could preemptively and mentally experience what was about to happen. Then, the "attitude-changing ritual" would begin. The old Navajo teacher grasped the fingers on the hand and lifted the paddle about a foot above the hand. Then, as fast as one of his Navajo arrows could fly into a target, the hand-warmer paddle would descend and smack the center of the palm.

I remember junior high school boys almost six feet tall with tears in their eyes, and their attitude about respecting boundaries instantly changed. Their newly found understanding is that you don't step over those boundaries. That Navajo teacher had just delivered a **Significant Life Experience (SLE)** that still lives inside my head today.

Nobody threatened to sue him, and no parents showed up at his doorstep claiming brutality. His job was to help young people understand the concept of boundaries. He succeeded.

He didn't break any bones or leave any scars. Boys from my junior high school grew up to be physicians, dentists, lawyers, and fathers of boys who presented new challenges in parenting to each one of them. I guess it's that mysterious chemical called "testosterone." Most boys don't know what to do with this chemical that is restructuring them from the inside out. Indeed, it kinda makes you go nuts. You do stupid things, say things you wish you could take back, and begin to act strange around girls... and your body stinks.

If the student didn't learn the S.L.E. lesson, it would "ratchet up" just a smidge. Three handwarmers would be delivered. After the first one, the student must recite these words: "Thank you sir. Please give me more."

The second hand warmer would fall from a little higher in the air. The muscles in the arm of the old Indian shop teacher would ripple just before the delivery. "Thank you, sir. Please give me more."

The last hand warmer would be the real S.L.E. lesson. "Thank you sir. I have learned my lesson."

Now, a hundred and fifty years later (or so it seems), the S.L.E. "Hand-warmer message delivered by the old Navajo still lives inside my head.

Do I think that was abuse? No, we didn't have any permanent injuries. We didn't have any parents running to the school saying look at my son's red hand. (The redness would be gone anyway.) And the vice principal would say, "Sure hope your son doesn't choose to do that again. Have a nice day."

I know all the excuses that bleeding heart liberals will come up with saying ,"That's cruel. That's terrible." "You should never do that to a child." But, even today, I remember the "Navajo Handwarmer."

It looks like the concept of higher education has changed...for the worse

Just take a look at what has happened to our educational institutions when liberals get hold of our kids, especially when they go to college. Suddenly, the concept of boundaries disappears because they've never really learned 'you don't do this.' That has become "A Curse on our Children."

So, in my head, when somebody steps over the boundaries, a part of me still says, "Man, that kid needs a "Navajo hand warmer." I can picture all of these spoiled college brats, lining up to get their "Navajo hand warmer" at Harvard, M.I.T., U.C.L.A. or other institutions of questionable "higher learning."

The "Navajo Hand Warmer therapy" should start with the university administrators who flash their degrees and forget to tell the world that they cheated on their dissertations and written examinations. Next in line are tenured, brainwashed full professors who think their "socialistic ideology" is more important than the transfer of knowledge on the subject matter. I would say that the entire university pecking order plus the ten thousand students should have this mental reset.

You're a Parent...you can be a friend later.

Parents must establish the concept of boundaries in their children's minds. Most importantly, parents must wake up and realize that we're cursing our kids if we don't teach them boundaries. We must teach them to respect boundaries, respect teachers, and respect the police. We must also realize that we're going through a giant social experiment, and everybody gets to play. How they play is really important.

What you see now with all these riots on college campuses, really twists my shorts. A significant change must happen.

Going to college may not be for everyone.

These liberal universities may have caused themselves so much damage that people with a brain are saying... "maybe my kids would do better in life if we save all that money. Maybe our family should travel the road less traveled and focus on an entirely different form of education rather than that *foofoo* university where the quasi-elite students act like spoiled brats that would trade their souls for a piece of parchment with symbolic words in raised letters.

Screaming, yelling, violently tearing up campuses, demanding "death to America" or one of our allies is <u>not</u> a sign of being educated. It's a sign of being brainwashed into an ideology that doesn't work and never will. It's a demand for "power" rather than "wisdom." Survival in this world depends on "wisdom" not "power." There will always be someone who is bigger and stronger. "Wisdom" wins.

Those of us with a normalized brain must believe that to deserve the "right" to be in this wonderful country of America, we've got to stop this crap and start learning to work together. If you don't get what you want, you still have no right to pick up a hammer and break in the glass at the university's front door. You don't.

A Parental "strong suggestion."

If you happen to be watching the evening news and see your precious little university student being sprayed in the face with police pepper spray and tearing things up, pick up your phone and call the student's cell phone, (that one that needs to be surgically removed from the side of his/her head) and tell your student to "get your fanny back to this house by tomorrow morning or I am permanently canceling your no limit, American Express card. You're done! We're changing the direction that you're going cause ...it ain't working... and you don't even know it."

It Takes Two to Dance...But It Only Takes One To Change The Dance...you're the parent!

If you're a parent and you don't do that, then you're a big part of the problem—in my humble opinion. We have lots of parents who are a big part of the problem, so parents, do your job.

<u>Message to parents or those who want to be parents:</u>

Here's a piece of reality just for parents: You're not there to be "best friends" with your children. You're there to be their "parents," and the main lesson that you teach him is that "boundaries are good" and that "boundaries are tight when you're very young." Once you see how they handle 'tight boundaries,' you spread the boundaries apart and give them more room to run. Incremental boundaries build responsible humans.

When your young people know and respect more boundaries, they have more freedom to experience more of life. When the brain has fully developed, the parent's job is done. At that point, you can become "their friend." Oh, you still pray for them and are there <u>if they ask for help</u>, be a coach, but at that point, you don't keep trying to parent them.

The world has a way of teaching young people important life lessons.   Young people are going to make mistakes. But, often, our biggest lessons come with the wrong choices we make. Hopefully, your young person will say, "Wow, I made a wrong turn. It's time for me to turn around and go a different path." They must reach that level of maturity without you (parents) forcing them.

When you observe your child return after making a bad life choice and decide to move down a different path, you can be proud because you've done what you're supposed to do as a parent. **Your job description is to be a parent. Don't be their friend because your job is to be their parent. They can get other friends. They can't get other parents.**

Now, here's your parental Navajo Handwarmer:

If you don't do your job as a parent, understand that you are hanging a Millstone around the necks of your children. You are cursing your children for a life of not understanding how to get along with people and live in a society that is supposed to be free. If kids don't learn the lessons from their parents, they go through life confused, and there will always be someone to say, "Hey, follow me." That person might lead them into a slavery that they may never escape.

Millstones are really, really heavy!

Chapter Eighteen

"Unjustice for All"

Chapter 6

"Unjustice for All"

<u>(A Satire of Reality)</u>

The courtroom buzzed with the low hum of guarded anticipation, the wooden benches packed with bloodthirsty spectators and journalists without cameras or microphones. At the bench, Judge Harold F. Grimstone, a feared and loathed figure, sat with imperious authority. His robe, as dark as his tattered Liberal soul, billowed slightly as he adjusted himself on his throne to rule over the darkened legal kingdom before him.

The district attorney, Marcus Vincent Viper, stood beside the bench, plumped with rolls of adipose stored in his neck, jowls, and around his girth, sporting a smirk playing at the corners of his lips. The theater performance of a lifetime was about to begin and the world was watching.

Their unholy alliance was an open secret, whispered about in hushed tones yet never openly challenged for fear of legal discipline. In this courtroom, Grimstone was god, and Viper was his hand servant. Actual guilt because of esoteric broken laws was just an option in this courtroom, but it was never required for conviction. Together, they spawned a formidable duo of corruption, wielding their power like a blunt instrument against the souls and fortunes of their helpless enemies captured by subpoena.

Today's target: former President Donald Stump. A man beloved by millions, Stump had once embodied the hopes of a nation, his tenure as President marked by economic prosperity, enhanced border security and a defiant stance against the establishment. Now, however, he was the victim of a meticulously orchestrated campaign of character assassination and legal entanglement designed to strip him of his dignity, financially cripple him, bind the time before the people, and effectively ruin his chance at a second term.

Judge Grimstone's gavel struck the wooden block with a resounding crack, silencing the murmurs in the gallery. He leaned forward, his steely gaze sweeping across the courtroom before settling on the defense table where Stump sat. His face was resolute and defiant but lined with weariness.

"Let us proceed," Grimstone growled, his voice dripping with this mockery of justice.

Viper, ever the opportunist, rose with a flourish of self-righteous indignation. "Your Honor, the case before us is not merely about one man's guilt but about the sanctity of our legal system. We have a man who has brazenly defied the rule of law, manipulated and corrupted for his own gain."

The irony was lost on no one. There was a district attorney whose own record was marred with scandals and backroom deals, now casting stones from within his own glass house. But the truth had no place in this courtroom; only the spectacle mattered.

As Viper continued his theatrical condemnation, Stump's attorneys, seasoned defenders of the wrongly accused, prepared for the inevitable uphill battle. They all knew the cards were stacked against them. Evidence had been fabricated, witnesses coerced, rehearsed, and offered the potential of reduced sentences for prior improprieties, and the jury was handpicked to ensure a predicted guilty verdict.

Judge Grimstone nodded approvingly at Viper's grandstanding, then turned his piercing eyes towards Stump. "Mr. Stump, how do you plead to these charges?"

Stump stood, his voice steady and clear. "Not guilty, Your Honor. These charges are a farce, a political witch hunt designed to keep me from serving the American people again."

Grimstone's lips curled into a sardonic smile. "We shall see if the evidence supports your claim."

Over the coming weeks, the courtroom became a *theater of the absurd*. Witnesses previously incarcerated because of their extensive history of lying, theft, pornography, and felonious misgivings instantly became fountains of truth, beacons of purity with criminal insight and unquestionable ethics, all focused against Stump. Veracity on the witness stand was only optional. Documents materialized out of thin air, all pointing to a vast conspiracy that only fools would believe. Yet, Grimstone and Viper reveled in their performance, knowing that their power shielded them from any accountability.

Viper called two witnesses from the darkest recesses of the Unjustice, themselves filled with the powers of hate and deceit, to provide the appearance of truth in the darkness of their fashioned reality.

First to the stand was Lester Mudge, a convicted and disbarred lawyer with a significant history of perjury in the courtroom and during testimony before Congress. But he was the default "star witness," so Viper's office conveniently overlooked his past penchant for lying. Mudge's eyes darted nervously around the courtroom as he took his oath, his hand visibly shaking. He had been promised leniency and protection in exchange for his testimony, a pact with the devil he now regretted but dared not defy.

"Mr. Mudge," Viper began, his voice smooth and insidious, "tell the court about your interactions with Mr. Stump."

Mudge licked his lips, his voice trembling. "I... I saw Mr. Stump intentionally mislead the public as he had me pay a ransom to Evelyn Jane Grimsby because of their alleged affair.   He said it was for his campaign, to ensure he got elected again."

Gasps erupted from the courtroom, though seasoned observers knew better. Mudge's tale was a patchwork of lies a fabrication born from the depth of desperation and coercion. Mudge was caught, but he had to move forward or else prove, once again, that his words had no truth. Yet it was just enough to sway the impressionable jury, their expressions turning to ones of horror and disdain.

Next, Viper called Evelyn Jane Grimsby, a woman whose loyalty to the Unjustice was as unshakable as her hatred for those who stood in its way. Grimsby was a master of manipulation and a queen of seduction who had honed her skills to a fine edge over years of staged sex before cameras and paying customers. Her silver tongue was adept at weaving the most intricate lies into seemingly irrefutable untruths.

"Evelyn," Viper addressed her with an almost intimate tone of carnal familiarity, "share with the court what you witnessed regarding Mr. Stump's dealings."

Grimsby leaned forward on the stand, her gaze cold, calculating, and filled with hate. "I personally witnessed Mr. Stump orchestrate a scheme to funnel illicit funds through shell companies. Following a very brief sexual encounter, and I do mean brief, Mr. Stump paid me well to keep it quiet. And he, through his attorney Lester Mudge, forced me to sign a Non-Disclosure Agreement (NDA)."

Her words were delivered with such conviction, such apparent sincerity, that the jury, growing weary from the tsunami of meaningless data thrown in their direction for a very long time, sat transfixed. They could not see the strings being pulled behind the scenes, the dark dual puppetry of Viper and Grimstone. They saw only what they were meant to see: a narrative crafted to destroy a man's reputation and political aspirations.

Throughout the testimonies, Stump sat stoically, his face a mask of calm defiance. Fatigue and relentlessly mounting anger were building within. He knew the game was being played, and the forces were amassed against him. With no legal choice, he endured the attack. He also knew that "truth" was fragile in the hands of the powerful and corrupt.

Grimstone watched the proceedings with a predatory gleam in his eyes. The courtroom was his domain, a theater where justice was but an illusion; defense objections were instantaneously overruled before entirely verbalized and twisted to serve his ambitions and those of his allies. As Viper wrapped up his questioning, the judge leaned forward, addressing the court with a voice dripping in *faux gravitas*.

"The testimonies we have heard today paint a damning picture of Mr. Stump's character and actions. It is clear that he poses a threat not only to our electoral process's integrity but also to the ethical fabric of our society."

Heavy with the weight of corruption, the courtroom buzzed with morbid fascination. They were witnessing the unjustified dismantling of a man's life, a spectacle orchestrated by the darkest forces within their well manipulated, dysfunctional justice system.

Outside the courthouse, the nation watched in disbelief. Stump supporters rallied in the streets, their chants of "Justice for Stump" echoing against the walls of an indifferent judicial system. They couldn't fathom the unjustified pain and twisted legality inflicted upon their presumptive chosen leader. Yet, Grimstone maintained the chokehold on Stump, dedicated to asphyxiating the last drop of life. In a surprise response, Stump supporters donated millions of dollars to the trapped candidate.

American citizens witnessed the unfolding travesty in their homes, a chilling reminder of how power could be corrupted to serve the darkest of purposes. The trial of Donald Stump was not just an attack on a man but an assault on the very principles of justice and democracy.

The jury, twelve people plus alternates, pulled from their productive professional lives, had been forced into Grimstone's service by a jury summons. They had to sort through meaningless evidence to prove a false assumption. Still, they were growing extremely tired and wanted to return to their lives of relative anonymity, but the case presented by Viper failed to be proven to the jurors.

They were at an impasse. Then the announcement came. At the end of a very long day, the jury's foreman sent a note to Judge Grimstone saying, "We have reached no conclusion. We can try again tomorrow." A disappointed and infuriated Grimstone, seated at the courtroom bench, announced to everyone, "The Jury is being sent home for the night without a verdict." A gasp rose from the defense and prosecutor's tables. Was this a hung jury or a predictor of an innocent eventuality?

Then, as if in a thriller movie's surprise ending, Judge Grimstone was handed a different note from the jury foreman: "I'm wrong; the jury has reached a verdict." Yet another gasp rose as the cacophony of mumbles was shocked at this fateful twist.

Judge Grimstone was now prepared to deliver the final fatal blow to Stump. He could already taste the sanguine triumph, envisioning the headlines that would follow. With Viper by his side, they had crafted a narrative so vile, so filled with evil hate, that even the most loyal supporters would question their faith because of the irreversible damage done to the concept of "Equal protection under the law" and the search for "truth" as the only expression of "justice."

With repressed glee, Grimstone read the 34 guilty counts against Stump. How could this be? Not one of the meaningless claims had been revealed by Grimstone and Viper until after the closing defense statements. Stump could not present a defense because defendants were prevented from knowing the charges being lodged against Stump. This legal sleight-of-hand had prevented Stump from a fair trial which would surely be overturned on appeal, but severe damage had been inflicted. Grimstone and Viper had been successful in branding an innocent man as a convicted felon, and this branding would serve to damage his reputation further and provide the liberal machine with what they needed to beat Stump into an anticipated political loss. America needed this man to save it from the evil forces launched against the ethical, moral, financial, and operational downfall of its society.

The rest of the story

What Grimstone, Viper, and powerful forces behind the scenes hadn't accounted for was the groundswell of "resilience," "truth" and the "power of the American people." As the gavel fell for the final time, an unexpected billowing tide of public outcry loudly emerged, determined to reclaim their country from the clutches of evil. Yet, in that moment, the seeds of a greater justice were sown, ones that would rise from the ashes of corruption and restore hope to a beleaguered nation.

The Media Accomplices

Even the incestuous media encampments, fully entrenched behind the forces of Grimstone and Viper, could almost taste the sanguine richness of the blood drops seeping from Stump's inflicted injuries. Polarized by decades of stigmatized and politicized reporting, hosts quite familiar with the passionate delivery of party verbiage breathlessly awaited the scripted unfolding of their supporting deceit cloaked as "News."

Under the harsh studio lights, media personalities sharpened their rhetoric, ready to echo and amplify the damning narratives spun in the courtroom. These hosts, masters of incendiary soundbites, had long abandoned any pretense of impartiality. Their shrouded allegiance to Grimstone and Viper was unwavering for fear that they might be the next victim in their crosshairs. Their broadcasts were a seamless extension of the courtroom's theatrics.

Each evening, as the sun set and the networks' prime-time slots approached, viewers were subjected to a barrage of venomous commentary. Pundits dissected Mudge and Grimsby's testimonies with glee, presenting them as irrefutable evidence of Stump's guilt. The airwaves crackled with condemnation; the carefully constructed lies reached millions of homes, embedding themselves into the collective consciousness of a nation already teetering on the edge of irreparable division.

"In tonight's top story," unfolded one anchor, her voice dripping with feigned concern, "we will delve deeper into the shocking revelations from Donald Stump's trial. What do these allegations mean for the future of our democracy?" Her eyes sparkled with malicious delight as she launched into a tirade against the former president, her words a carefully choreographed dance of character assassination as a precursor to political death.

In another studio, a roundtable of experts nodded sagely, their discussion a parade of half-truths and speculative fiction no longer bound by the need for multiple source testing prior to birth on air. "Stump's corruption was boundless," one commentator declared, "He treated the presidency like his personal playground. We can only hope the judiciary will deliver the justice our nation deserves."

The narrative was unyielding, relentlessly hammering to break Stump's supporters' will and discredit dissenting voices. Even as the courtroom drama unfolded, the media ensured that the public perception was tightly controlled, any semblance of nuance or fairness drowned out by the drumbeat of condemnation.

Yet, amidst the cacophony, a growing resistance began to stir. Independent journalists and alternative media outlets, undeterred by the mainstream's stranglehold, started questioning the official story. They dug into the backgrounds of Mudge and Grimsby, uncovering the cracks in their testimonies and the shadowy deals orchestrated by Viper. They highlighted the glaring inconsistencies and the blatant collusion between the judiciary and the media. Yet the untouchable

Federal Judge beamed with glee at the thought of his courtroom trophy.

On social media platforms, hashtags like #JusticeForStump and #ExposeTheTruth began trending, drawing attention to the miscarriage of justice before the nation's eyes. Livestreams from rallies, where supporters of Stump gathered to voice their outrage, garnered millions of views. Millions of dollars flowed into Stump's re-election coffers. The grassroots movement swelled, fueled by a collective determination to reclaim their narrative from the clutches of corruption.In the courtroom, Stump's defense attorney seized upon this burgeoning momentum. "Ladies and gentlemen of the jury," he began in his closing statement, "what we have witnessed here is not justice. It is a carefully orchestrated charade designed to destroy a man who dared to stand against the establishment. The evidence against my client is fabricated, the witnesses compromised, and the media complicit. Do not be swayed by the spectacle. Look at the facts, and you will see the truth."

Unjustice for All

At that moment, the trial of Donald Stump became more than just a legal proceeding. It became a symbol of the struggle for the divided soul of a nation, a battle between the forces of corruption and the indomitable spirit of a people yearning for true justice. Within the recesses of thought, many realized...'if this could happen to Stump...it could happen to any American.'

And then the worm turned.

Many miles away, in the heart of the capital, locked behind impenetrable pillars of alabaster, the last bastion of law was at work. Combing through layers of truth, history, and the intent of our forefathers, the black-robed defenders of the true American spirit sought wisdom for our country. When the opinion was released to the nation, Grimstone and Viper were shaken to their very core.

American citizens will not accept the forced imposition of "Unjustice for All." The seeds of truth sewn by patriots long gone will rise from their hallowed graves. America, Truth, and Justice shall all reunite when the sun rises once again.

Chapter Nineteen

Hostages

Chapter 7

<u>"Hostages"</u>

Many believe they understand what the word "Hostage" means. When you look at the Merriam-Webster dictionary, this is the definition where we must start. **"a person held by one party in a conflict as a pledge pending the fulfillment of an agreement; a person taken by force to secure the taker's demands"; and "one that is involuntarily controlled by an outside**

influence." ("Hostage." Merriam-Webster.com Dictionary, Merriam-Webster, .)

America was born on July 4, 1776, making us 247 years old. This seems really old, but it's not when you consider the age of the Bible: 1500 years old. The stories about "hostages" are found throughout the Bible.

"Significant change" in the history of civilizations often happens when its people reach a 'breaking point' and feel they are being held "hostage" by rules, laws, societal injustice, or physical force to which they cannot and will not agree as "acceptable." When the essential "spirit" of the American people has been violated, becoming unquestionably immoral, illegal, or fundamentally destructive to the life-giving essence that holds society together, "change" happens.

In my opinion, America and Americans have reached that "breaking point" under the rule of President Joe Biden, Vice President Harris, and a powerful Liberal Democrat regime that has chosen to "rule" rather than "represent" to "force change that benefits only those in power," while disregarding the totality of American citizens and the laws that have been created over the last 274 years that give "structure" to the "reality" of being an American.

The current regime has created chaos in our peace-loving society to hide a severe cancer being nurtured in secret behind closed doors. In short, there are tens of millions of Americans who feel they are being held "hostage," and anyone who disagrees with the ruling government cartel is expendable as a necessary casualty of the social conflict.

It sounds like socialism. It is. The problem is this: This is not an America that can survive all that is being forcibly pushed on its citizens. Throughout history, socialism has never worked, except for the ruling party. Everyone else is expected to adapt and get used to having less of everything. **Reality: equal misery under the rule of law. That's not America.**

These are just a few of the symptoms of a very sick American patient/system currently in place:

1. Americans have been subjected to a tsunami of illegal aliens breaching the borders of our country, bringing diseases, social pathology, willful use of violence on our legal American citizens, destruction of private property, and creating a social imbalance in our country that is absolutely unsustainable.

2. Americans have experienced rule-by-edict, with President Joe Biden, VP Harris, and the unethical Liberal Democrat party wiping away the legally created laws of Congress that have protected America and Americans for decades, creating a voting imbalance that would perpetuate Liberal Democrat electoral dominance. Fearfully, the next evolution of this predictive pathology will be an edict that makes millions of illegal aliens (or more) instantly into American citizens beholding to Liberal Democrats for this edict, with the expected *Quid Pro Quo* that they will all become **voting Liberal Democrats.**

3. Americans have watched our economy ripped to shreds by out-of-control spending with no intention of ever paying back the debt created by this regime. This creates hostages for every man, woman, and child for decades into the future, as we must balance debt with the growth of our gross national production.

4. Americans have observed the Executive Branch of govern-

ment under President Biden/Harris and Liberal Democrats to ignore the Judicial Branch of our Government. Following the findings of the Supreme Court is not an option; it is the law, and...as we often hear, "No one is above the Law."

5. Americans have experienced mental instability that seriously questions the wisdom of handing the key to our nuclear launch systems to President Biden or Vice President Harris. They work as one even though the incompetency of VP Harris exceeds that of President Biden.

6. The fact that the American public blatantly observes at least two forms of justice indicates that there is currently no uniform standardization of justice any longer in America. Lady Liberty no longer wears a blindfold; she now wears either a Democrat T-shirt or has been defiled with a flag from another country. Our concept of equal protection under the law has been thrown out the window between the Obama and Biden administrations. Murders, rapists, gangs involved in the active insurrection of our country are not held to justice. They are released back into society to commit the same acts repeatedly. This is morally and ethically wrong, but it continues to be endorsed by those currently in power over our government.

7. One significant observational disappointment is that Liberal Democrats, under the guise of being in the majority, have enabled the continued destruction of America. What has become apparent is that America is for sale, and the Biden Administration is the broker. The Biden family and "The Big Guy" get rich off each transaction as America is repeat-

edly damaged.

8. Losing a major portion of our strategic oil reserves with no intention to rebuild these reserves means we are vulnerable if attacked. Our refusal to allow drilling of our subterranean oil deposits, selling oil to our enemies, and then buying oil needed for gas production from our enemies means that we are selling America short, and our people are paying dearly because of this ideology push that moves opposite to the regular market forces that help us in a market-driven economy.

9. Most of America is observing a death event. But it's not the death of America; it's the death of Democrat Liberalism as it has been forced on this country. American citizens will not stand for this slavery on its people.

A man...or a horse?

There is an old story about a man walking down the street when he encounters a longtime friend who asks him, "How are you feeling?" The man responds, "I feel great. Why?"

"Because you're beginning to look a lot like my horse."

The man walks down the street and encounters another old friend. The discussion goes about the same. "I feel great. Why?"

The friend responds, "Because you're looking like a horse."

The man thinks it's strange that his friends would say those things but makes an appointment with his doctor. After a short wait in the reception room, the man enters the examination room to meet with his doctor.

"Sir, as your doctor, I want you to be healthy and happy ...and you know you can trust me. How can I help you?"

"Doc, do I look like a horse?"

At about that time, the doctor's cell phone rang. He quickly grabbed the buzzing phone and answered it preparing to leave the examination room the doctor said, "Sir, you'll have to excuse me. I must take this emergency call, but don't worry, everything is fine."

Before leaving the room, the doctor turned to his nurse and said, "I have to take this call. Can you please bring this patient a bucket of fresh oats, a couple of carrots, and get him a referral to the veterinarian across the street?"

We can't keep America with our eyes wide shut.

Sometimes, others see things we have never noticed or refuse to allow ourselves to see. But often, our elected representatives begin to believe that the citizens are just plain stupid. They think we will always eat the "bucket of oats" they give us. They're wrong.

I can't recall the Liberal Democrat who said this, but it seems like every Liberal Democrat in Washington has received and memorized a copy of this memo: **"Keep telling the public lies, and eventually, they will begin to believe it's true."**

Never Underestimate the enemy, even if the enemy is your brother.

One of the first rules of combat training is to "never underestimate the enemy." The hardest part of recognizing the enemy is that they often look like usual, everyday Americans. They use the right words and have the proper titles, but they hide the most dastardly destructive motives to use against other Americans.

Presidents, vice presidents, and the President's cabinet should be the best, top-flight, intelligent experts on the responsibilities of their office from across the United States. No tokens. However, right now the actions of these key people show that the president, VP, and Cabinet are not representing America's best interests. Because of their actions, it is apparent that this administration should be terminated from their jobs as quickly as possible. Certainly, they should not be elected for another term!

Any one of these egregious acts we've covered in seven chapters would justify immediate termination. If this were a 1200-page book, I would run out of pages before I would run out of termination topics with the same conclusion. And, here's a concept that needs immediate passage: **when someone in our government (elected or appointed) lies, they are immediately terminated and relinquish the totality of their retirement funds. No exceptions.**

Turning Point

As hard as it is to express this opinion, here we go. In my opinion: America is at a moral and ethical "turning point" for survival. It sounds cataclysmic, but it's true: Either bedrock Americans change administrations at the ballot box, or America as we know it may not survive.

Merriam-Webster defines a "turning point" as A point at which a change must be made.

If you knew that your vote in the upcoming election could determine whether our country survives ...or not, how would you vote? Your vote in this next election cycle <u>is just that important</u>. How you vote will reverberate our American worth throughout the rest of the world and to generations of Americans yet unborn.

Chapter Twenty

Hostages (SPLIT)

<u>Commentary by Dr. Ulyses Stuckum</u>

"Things I may not understand about life"

One day, while I was in the frenzy of putting together my new practice in a beautiful West Texas town, I got a call from the Assistant Chief of the town police department. The whole department had 15 officers.

I still remember walking into his office and seeing a large poster of **Officer Barny Fife** from the old ***Andy Griffith TV show*** **in the** town of Mayberry proudly hung on the wall as the epitome of police interaction with the public. When I asked him about the poster, he said, "He's my idol, and someday I pray that our little department can touch as many lives as he did." There was almost "innocence" in his voice.

"Doc, we sure appreciate you setting up a shop in our little town, and I know our hospital needs you. Out here, we have been protected from some of the bad stuff that goes on in the big cities, but I'm afraid it's quickly finding us."

I told him, "People are people wherever you go. The best you can do is help them know when they have crossed the line. But I'm sure your officers are doing the best they can."

"We've got a lot of folks that pass through here on the major highway. Many of them work in oil and gas, but they come from everywhere. Our little town bank has a sign that shows the up-to-the-minute price for a barrel of crude."

"I think that's a first for me. But that's how they survive, so it's information they need."

"It's a first for lots of folks passing through."

"Doc, I need your help, but this should be between you and me."

"I'm pretty good at keeping secrets."

"We've picked up on something that could be pretty significant for our little town. You know we are not very far from the border, which means we get some big-city crime. We have a couple of apartment units with 50 or so individual apartments each.

"One of my guys has picked up on a possible child trafficking operation, and we're going to go in on a raid. The judge gave us the search warrants, and we are almost ready. I would like you to go with us 'cause we don't know what's inside that apartment, and we may need your help for any victims."

"What made you think it was child trafficking?"

"It's on the third floor of the apartment building, and on the front porch, large sacks of used children's clothing and other items we found. It's much more than is possible for a 3-bedroom apartment with one or even two families. And, a steady stream of men in and out of that apartment, day and night"

"Sounds pretty logical."

"My guys really use their heads pretty well. Will you go in with us on this raid?"

"You bet."

"When?"

"Tonight. I've got body armor you can wear."

"I appreciate that. What time do you want me here?"

"At ten PM, we'll meet here at the station and get briefed."

At 9:30, I showed up and put on my body armor. They introduced me, and their faces showed that they were glad I was there. The assistant chief introduced me to the sergeant on the force longest.

"Doc, stick to this Seargent and listen to him. He ain't fast, but if he ever catches someone, they ain't getting away. We go in first, and then you come in after the takedown."

The little police force arrived without lights or sirens. They went up three flights of stairs. Everyone was in position. The sergeant knocked loudly on the door, and it opened. The sergeant announced, "Police," and pushed open the door as all the officers, sidearms drawn, entered the apartment.

I have to say I don't think the officers were ready for what they saw. I know I wasn't.

Six cages had been constructed out of chicken wire and wooden pallets. Each had doors on them with hinges and locks. Inside the cages were children from 5 to 9 years of age. The look of horror had captured their faces. The officers took the adults in the room to the floor, got handcuffs on them, and took them to the waiting police step van.

There was trauma everywhere. For a moment after the adult traffickers were secured and removed, I began to assess the emotional and physical trauma in the room and triaged my response. The officers removed the children one by one. Fathers and mothers who were officers could be seen instinctively hugging their captive children and whispering, "You're safe," "I've got you," and "Those bad guys are gone."

It was easy to see that there were three sets of victims at that crime scene: the captive children, the police officers, and... me. Each officer took his/her captive child to their police car, and in a caravan, we headed to the hospital. The officers chose to stay with their captive child as long as possible during the examination. At the appropriate time, they left the room while the ER team handled the exam and established their own triage of the little victims.

After the children were safe, I focused on the police officers. One of the officers told me that when he opened the cage and looked into the face of the child, he said, "The face I saw was the face of my own child. I thought I was saving... my own child."

The trauma had affected each one of the officers, their spouses, and their children in totally different ways. When the news broke, the wave of trauma spread like a never-ending circular wave responding to a very large boulder being dropped in the center of a previously still pond.

The other reality I still live with today is that normal humans cannot avoid experiencing a deep emotional response to an event like this. It changes people forever, regardless of age, gender, or political inclination. Trauma like this is nothing short of having a bucket of black ink poured into the emotional spirit of each person who experiences it. It's ink that can never be extracted. It can only be partitioned in the brain by extensive psychotherapy and emotional support.

When I examine a child with an earache or runny nose, sometimes my thoughts go back to those children in the cages that night.

Critical incident Stress Management and CISM Debriefing, delivered by an experienced team of professionals, can help the officers and all who know them. Some officers, after this type of experience or the experience of being forced to use their weapon in a deadly encounter, cannot handle it and choose to leave police work for other gainful employment.

People who are involved in Child Sex Slavery as a captor or a customer...are sick...really sick!

There are abnormal people who can justify trafficking children for daily or hourly sex use, just like renting a tool or object for a project. As far as those who offer children for sexual abuse or those who rent them, I feel confident that there will be an eternal interaction with the Creator of the Universe that all begins with that heavy millstone, but I believe that's just the beginning.

An estimated 448,000 children arrived on the Southern Border of the United States.

What parents would have their children dangerously walk across Mexico to reach the US Border...alone or unaccompanied by a parent? These children often have the bare essentials for life on this journey: a gallon of water, a little food, and a cell phone. Who brings them, if not a parent or family member?

Most of us don't want to think that parents would turn their children over to coyotes that transport them to the border where the Border Patrol Officers and ICE Agents take them in

and register them. In a recent news release, the quantity of Illegal migrants/aliens has exploded to such massive numbers that there is no place for them to go in America. CBS Austin just ran a story showing 30,000 children were lost. Now a government report shows that it's over 300,000 children that have been processed at the border and released into America...but cannot be found. Inside America's border states, the child sexual traffickers are waiting. And, these helpless little ones are given food, water and a cage. Welcome to America...you are now a slave .

Of all of the emotional pathologies found in this liberal democrat Biden/Harris administration, this is the worst, in my opinion. Yet, Democrats go into Chicago, smile, laugh, collect, and spend large sums of money to fund the perpetual re-election...while this type of human carnage takes place. 30,000 kids lost inside America...those words are deafening. Stop all the other non-essential stuff and find those children. I don't understand how there can be any other option.

We must do better at protecting our children of all ages from all sorts of "emotional ink" that can stain their little hearts and minds forever. What can you say to a child who has lost their innocence for life after being sexually trafficked? Protecting the Border and improving respect for our police officers is just the beginning. That's our responsibility as Americans and as humans.

If our prosecutors and DAs put the criminals back out on the street without prosecution, I suggest matching 'millstones' for the criminals and the guilty prosecutors/DAs. Don't let them hurt Americans anymore.

America has survived many traumatic injuries over 270 years. But this year seems to be different, unique, and very frightening. This is not just another election. Liberal Democrats have repeated the cliche, "Elections have consequences." So true. How we relate to our country affects our perception of happiness in our lives and the lives of our families. If oppressed, we experience what is going on in other countries.

What difficult questions should you ask yourself before voting in the next election?

Because we are emotional creatures, it is difficult, if not impossible, to think with total logic and withhold emotion. When considering which party to vote for or which individual to vote for, think about what that person or party has done in the past to create freedom and protection for America. The past actions of someone are a pretty important predictor of what they will do in the future.

Pick the surgeon you want operating on you.

There is a story about a man lying on a gurney, ready to be rolled into the operating room for a very serious surgery. The OR nurse arrives in Pre-Op and speaks to the man on the gurney.

"Sir, in this hospital, we do things a little differently than in other hospitals. Just before going into this life-changing surgery, we give you a last-minute chance to choose the surgeon you want to cut you open and fix your problem."

"Nurse, they already gave me my pre-operative sedation and I'm pretty sleepy. My eyes don't focus very well, but in this condition, how can I make this decision?"

"Sir, this is your chance to vote. You have a right to choose the doctor you want save your life, but once you choose, you're stuck with that choice for all treatment for the next four years. Now choose."

"Can someone else make this choice for me?"

"Sir, since you have blurred vision and are somewhat emotional, let me tell you a little about these two teams of surgeons."

"The Doctor on your right is a highly trained surgeon with 30 years of experience and boarded in this specialty. He's performed thousands of these procedures. The patients love him. When he gives a lecture, sometimes 10-15,000 people show up. His name is Dr. Stump. Assisting him will be Dr. DVance. They've reviewed your records and X-rays. And they really work together well. They're all scrubbed up and ready to go."

"The other Doctor just received her medical degree from a school in California, no residency or fellowship, and we understand that she really tore up the school and left it in a mess when she moved to Washington...and last night she had a pretty late night at a local bar Now, she tends to cackle when she's nervous and doesn't know what to say, but you'll be asleep, so the cackling won't bother you as much as it bothers <u>every other human who has worked with her.</u>"

"She has nobody to assist her in surgery. She had some assistants, but they all quit because she's a pain in the ass who thinks she can do any surgery...but has no experience. I heard she was assigned to work in a hospital down on the Southern Border of the United States. Her name is Dr. Somala Paris. Her friends call her "the border czar"...but she keeps denying that she was ever assigned to handle the border patients. Problem is...she just never showed up. We're lucky she showed up here for this surgery, but you know, she has to look the part...she's never really done."

"Ok so, what's your choice. We only have the operating room so long. Sir, wake up...also, if you choose her... you'll have to put in your own catheter."

"I can't make a decision on this."

"Well, most people just close their eyes and roll the dice. If it's snake eyes...you get Somala. Any other number, and you get Doctor Stump. Just between you and me, I would pray for the Stump DVance team...if you want to get well."

I think the man rolled the dice, got double 6's...and lived happily ever after.

"Hope" and "Change" don't solve the problems of America.

"Hope and change" is more than a comedian with a pocket of coins. "Hope" has nothing to do with the past conduct of a political candidate. Each American has a duty and responsibility to choose the best and the brightest person for each job. Being a "token" of any kind has nothing to do with your ability to handle really difficult decisions that might involve stopping world wars, and protecting a few hundred million people on the face of this planet...or not.

In this election, possibly like never before, Americans must be voting to remove their citizens from being "hostages." Lies with no productive and preventive action could enslave Americans for generations. Fiscal irresponsibility results in a panoply of bad choices. This is the moment we define who we really are. Do we protect our America, or do we hand it over to those who will spend it into oblivion, redefine the morals and ethics fine-tuned by hundreds of years of American history. Did the blood of our sons and daughters shed our liberty, mean anything? Or do we hand America over to those who have no love for America but who want to use it, abuse it, and discard our precious homeland as trash.

This is our moment to define who we are and what our country will be in the future. America is worth our full dedication to recapturing our heritage.

Vote in this election as though your life and your loved ones' lives depended on the outcome... because that may be the case!

Chapter Twenty-One

Epilogue

Epilogue

Today is Sunday, July 14, 2024, and Americans across the globe are still in shock at the attempted assassination of Donald J. Trump, the 45th President of the United States. Was it a "twist of fate" that The President was looking to the right when the gunman decided to pull the trigger, instantaneously sending the bullet intended for the brain to miss and pass through a portion of his ear?

As an ordained police chaplain, I don't put much faith in statements like a "twist of fate." I prefer a much more accurate term. I believe this was a clear-cut act of "divine intervention" where the Creator showed through His actions that Trump's death was not the path that history must record. As Paul Harvey would say about now, what comes next is "the rest of the story."

Throughout my life, I have often seen the Creator of the Universe (and all universes) reach over the portal of eternity and reverse a logical conclusion that we humans believe was merely "fate." Trust me, I am not trying to deify Donald Trump in any way. He is not perfect, but none of us are. Imperfect people can still be selected to do great things on this earth for humans. I believe Donald J. Trump is a man on a mission.

"Miracles happen... when they're supposed to." That's a line I wrote long ago for a Christmas Drama screenplay. Right now, we need to be reminded of that simple message. God does not dole out miracles just to billionaires, ministers, or the upper class (whoever that may be); miracles are given to every one of us every day. When you take your next breath, that's a miracle. When you lay on your bed with a broken body riddled with cancer and take your last breath, finding yourself before the gates of Eternity for an up close and personal chat with God, having left that broken body behind... that's a miracle.

For so many who don't recognize miracles, death seems to be the ultimate end. Many who sit in artificially created positions of political power dole out different versions of "death" on others to prove superiority over a human. That's **politics.**

In the life of Donald J. Trump, we have watched on TV uncontrolled, hate-driven prosecutors and Judges twisting human laws to perform dastardly acts intended to take the "monetary life" of this imperfect man. We've watched on television hate-driven prosecutors and Judges make unthinkable accusations to take the "emotional life" of this imperfect man. That's **politics.**

We've watched on TV biased, incendiary media power brokers, both in front and behind the news cameras, throw media ethics out the window, having given up the concept of ethical reporting of facts to take away this imperfect man's "public persona life," but he keeps on keeping on. That's **politics,** too.

All of these attacks on sub-parts of Trump's life are perpetrated because of "politics" and the quest for the perception of superiority while proving human inferiority.

It was only a natural progression of human hate layered upon itself many times, that eventually, someone would attempt an actual assassination of the physical life of this imperfect man...on TV... a few days before a national political convention, only to find out that a man on a mission of protecting America...is not going to be an easy target. Bullets are no match for God and what He wants done.

Americans worldwide must consciously decide that 'boundaries of behavior' are vital for perpetuating bedrock American values. Enforce those boundaries so your kids don't grow up confused. If those boundaries are not infused into each human's emotional DNA, trust me, they will seek various unethical and immoral ways to position themselves in society. That is also termed **"Politics."**

So, dust off that Bible and start sharing with your children (of any age) the secrets of life hidden in those pages. The "Ten Commandments" are not 'suggestions' from afar. If people don't know the rules, they start making them up themselves. That creates confusion and chaos about how to live a happy life with a few billion people across the earth. That is the real definition of .... (You fill in the blank.)

It doesn't matter if you live in Ukraine, Russia, Nigeria, or West Texas, USA. When you choose leaders who look out for themselves more than they do for the people they supposedly represent, you often hear, "Now <u>that</u> makes me mad." That's a sign that it's time for a change through casting honest ballots. It's time to make that vote and let the world know 'change is on the way.'

And you wonder why I named this book **"Now That Makes Me Mad**[sm]**...about Politics?"**

Dr. Keith A. Robinson

*****END*****